SUÁREZ

About the author

Luca Caioli is the bestselling author of *Messi, Ronaldo* and *Neymar*. A renowned Italian sports journalist, he lives in Spain.

SUÁREZ

THE EXTRAORDINARY STORY BEHIND
FOOTBALL'S MOST EXPLOSIVE TALENT

Updated Edition

LUCA CAIOLI

ICON

This updated edition first published in the UK in 2015 by Icon Books Ltd

Previously published in the UK and USA in 2014 by
Icon Books Ltd, Omnibus Business Centre,
39–41 North Road, London N7 9DP
email: info@iconbooks.com
www.iconbooks.com

Sold in the UK, Europe and Asia
by Faber & Faber Ltd, Bloomsbury House,
74–77 Great Russell Street, London WC1B 3DA or their agents

Distributed in the UK, Europe and Asia
by TBS Ltd, TBS Distribution Centre, Colchester Road
Frating Green, Colchester CO7 7DW

Distributed in Australia and New Zealand
by Allen & Unwin Pty Ltd, PO Box 8500,
83 Alexander Street, Crows Nest, NSW 2065

Distributed in South Africa
by Jonathan Ball, Office B4, The District,
41 Sir Lowry Road, Woodstock 7925

Distributed in India by Penguin Books India,
7th Floor, Infinity Tower – C, DLF Cyber City, Gurgaon 122002, Haryana

Distributed in Canada by Publishers Group Canada,
76 Stafford Street, Unit 300, Toronto, Ontario M6J 2S1

Distributed to the trade in the USA by
Consortium Book Sales and Distribution,
The Keg House, 34 Thirteenth Avenue NE,
Suite 101, Minneapolis, Minnesota 55413-1007

ISBN: 978-190685-097-5

Typeset in New Baskerville by Marie Doherty

Printed and bound in the UK by Clays Ltd, St Ives plc

Contents

Chapter 1
A powerful identity

José Mujica is not a great lover of football. As a kid, as with all kids, he played football but at twelve he started to cycle and for three or four seasons, he dedicated all his time to cycling. He supports Atlético Cerro because it is the team where he lives and because when he was younger, Huracán del Paso de la Arena did not exist.

He is not a great lover of the 'sphere' but he knows that in Latin America, 'the greatest form of communication is football which, together with language, is the strongest bond and relationship which can exist between societies in South America. A simple game has become something of the utmost seriousness and importance.' A game which some-times leads to violence in the stadiums: 'the beast within us which threatens the heart of all societies'. Leaving violence to one side, Mujica is convinced that 'Uruguay is one of the most football obsessed countries in the world.' In a recent radio interview, he commented: 'Relative to the size of the country and the potential of each citizen [there are 3.3 mil-lion people in Uruguay], Uruguayan football is a miracle created by the passion of our people.'

The nation's former President, who from 2010 to 2015 sur-prised the world with his laws (legalisation of marijuana, abor-tion and gay marriage) and his recipe for human happiness (as reported on by *The Economist* which awarded the country Country of the Year 2013), is right. He is not the only one to think like this. The footballing miracle is the topic of conversation in all circles of society: facts, numbers and statistics are trotted out to prove this by anyone you ask. The four stars on the light blue shirt of the national team remind the populace of the two Olympic golds (1924 and 1928) and the two World Cups (1930 and 1950); there were also fifteen Copa Americas. The generalised practice and routine of football: from the dusty side streets to the lush green pitches of the professional teams, from the streets to 'baby football' (every weekend Montevideo sees around 3,000 matches of baby football being played, a real social event for the families and the kids aged between five and twelve.) The national championship, across the first and second divisions, has 34 clubs, 29 of which are in the capital. The tickets to go and watch the matches are reasonable: 80 to 500 pesos (€2.50–15). This allows anyone who wants to go and watch a game. All of these matches are viewed for peanuts compared to the European figures: US$10 million for the TV rights in Uruguay compared to €1,229 million for the Premier League; US$15 million is the budget for Club Nacional against €520 million for Real Madrid. Pepe Mujica commented: '[This last figure] is probably an amount which Uruguayan football has not spent in its entire history'. And yet notwithstanding the money and the numbers, the footballing miracle continues and the tiny South American country fights its corner amidst the giants of Brazil and Argentina. It can boast a whole host of magical players as though it were a nation of 60 or 200 million inhabitants. Why? Because football is a passion (or illness) which runs through the veins of society at all levels. Because it is a country with weak national identity, where nationalism is not valued strongly and where national pride is placed in the light blue shirt and in *antiporteñismo* (anti-Argentine sentiment). Football is a powerful identity: a substantial and fundamental part of the culture of the nation. And it is getting even more powerful as it defines the role that sport and football plays in the value system of the nation. There is a real symbiosis between football and the country. Uruguay stops for two events and two events only: a national match and the general elections. Politics and football are central to life in the Eastern Republic of Uruguay. So much so that the list of Uruguayan heroes is peppered with footballers like Obdulio Varela, 'El Negro Jefe', who played in the 1950 World Cup and José Nasazzi, 'El Mariscal', who played in the 1930 World Cup. Football is the place where conflicts are played out, where great discourse is made and the source of the expressions which infiltrate the language: '*Los de afuera son de palo*' ('Outsiders don't play'). This was the phrase which Varela famously said to boost his team's morale before entering Maracanã packed with 200,000 fans. It is a phrase used to indicate that those who are outside the family, the group or the party do not count. It is better not to listen to the outsiders.

How this world was built, this powerful identity, has to do with the history of the Eastern Republic of Uruguay, even though it is hard to work out even today.

Football everywhere, as in Brazil, Argentina, Italy, Germany and France, is connected to the industrial revolution and the expansion of the English economy. It was Her Majesty Queen Victoria's subjects who spread sport to every corner of the globe. Football arrived at the port of Montevideo in the luggage of the sailors, craftsmen, professors, workers, bank managers, railway personnel and gas company workers. At the end of the nineteenth century it came and got a foothold at the cricket clubs like Montevideo Cricket Club, founded in 1861.

The members of the club played not only in their whites and with their bats made of cork and leather but started to play rugby and football against teams from the merchant ships and the Royal Navy. One such match took place in 1878 along the coast near Carretas Point.

But the records show that it was only in 1881, on 22 June, that the first official match between two clubs from Montevideo took place. The match was played in the La Blanqueada quarter on a pitch which the English called the English Ground. The Montevideo Cricket Club against the Montevideo Rowing Club. The final score was 1-0 to the cricketers. Seven days later the rematch: the Cricket Club won again, 2-1. It was the Montevideo Cricket Club which hosted the first international match, on 15 August 1889, against the Argentinians of Buenos Aires Cricket Club. The locals watched the new pastime of the crazy English with detached bemusement but bit by bit the younger members of well-to-do society in Montevideo started to get hooked.

From behind his desk in his office just a stone's throw from the stadium's Amsterdam stands, Mario Romano, manager of the Centenary Stadium of Montevideo, explained: 'In May of 1891, Enrique Cándido Litchenberger sent an invite to his schoolmates at the English High School to set up a Uruguayan football club. On 1 June 1891, it was done. The Football Association was set up and played its first match in August against the Montevideo Cricket Club. In September, the club changed its name to Albion Football Club in honour of the birthplace of football.'

It is clear to see that England was the inspiration for many clubs in the Eastern Republic, as for example the footballers of the College of Capuchin Monks. In 1915, they were looking for a name for their club and they took inspiration from the map of the United Kingdom. They remembered the explanations of their teacher in class: the students were taught that huge transatlantic cargo ships left from the port of Liverpool headed for Montevideo. After hearing this, they were in no doubt and decided to call their club 'Liverpool'. The team still plays today in the second division. It is also worth considering the origins and diatribe of Uruguayan football which even today have not been agreed upon. It lies somewhere in the history of Nacional and Peñarol, the rivalry between the most important clubs in the country; the teams have won 93 of the 110 titles between them, plus eight Libertadores Cups and six Intercontinental Cups. On 14 May 1889, Club Nacional de Football was born from the merger of two university clubs (Montevideo Football Club and Uruguay Athletic Club de La Unión). Club Nacional de Football, the answer to the colonial teams. This is the reason the strip of the club is white, light blue and red, the same as the flag of José Gervasio Artigas, the father of the Uruguayan nationhood.

On 28 September 1891, in the north-eastern part of Montevideo, a group of mainly English workers from the Central Uruguay Railway Company of Montevideo Limited, formed the Central Uruguay Railway Cricket Club, known as CURCC or, for short, Peñarol (a name which comes from the area in the north-east of the city where the railway companies' building yards were). Their colours were yellow and black like the railway signals. It was here that CURCC started to make its mark on the Uruguayan championship. In 1900, CURCC met three other teams, Albion, Deutscher and Uruguay Athletic in the Uruguayan championship. On 13 December 1913, CURCC officially renamed itself Peñarol. CURCC had played at least 50 matches against Nacional: *Carboneros* (colliers) vs *Bolsos* (pockets, as they used to play with a jersey that had a pocket on the chest), Peñarol vs Nacional; on the one side the English railway club, on the other the university elite; on the one hand the *gringos*, on the other the nationalistic elite. It was this rivalry that formed the backdrop to football in the salad days of the Eastern Republic. It was there that the passion for this beautiful game started to fill the veins of the nation. The sport spread like wildfire engulfing a generation of young men as it went. Other teams sprouted: Wanderers, River Plate, Bristol, Central, Universal, Colon, Reformers, Dublin ...

Matches were played against English teams such as Southampton, Nottingham Forest and Tottenham who were on tour in South America. The eternal rivalry between Argentina and Uruguay got under way in the Lipton Cup and Newton Cup.

Football was a social leveller. It was a place where the poor and rich could integrate and mix; immigrants mixed with the well-to-do. Between 1860 and 1920, Uruguay saw a mass influx of immigrants from Europe – Spain and Italy mainly – which changed the demographics of the country for ever. This European immigration was matched by the influx of African Brazilians, slaves in some cases, coming from nearby Brazil. The mixed-race population was key to the composition of Uruguayan society. In a country without serious inter-class tensions and where there aren't deep-rooted aristocratic tendencies, immigrants, Africans and Hispanics are muddled together.

Lincoln Maiztegui Casas, history professor and author of epic political and social studies in Uruguay which cover the very beginnings of socio-political trends in Uruguay, explained the demographics as follows: 'At the start of the 1900s, Uruguay was not an egalitarian society but it was integrated thanks to the experience of a social state and the education system reform in 1877 promoted by José Pedro Varela. School was non-religious, free and mandatory. The idea that a rich person's son and a poor person's son could go to the same school, use the same pinafore and same bow was born. It was a reform which created a surge for equality in society and slowly eroded the cultural differences between the indigenous population and the immigrants. The immigrants did not lose touch with their cultural roots but deep in their soul they feel Uruguayan.'

Football played the same role in helping to bring people from different cultures and classes together. You only need to take a look at the names of the national team which won the Paris Olympics in 1924, i.e. Petrone, Scarone, Romano, Nasazzi, Iriarte and Urdinaran, and you realise that the majority of the names are Italian and Spanish in origin. There was José Leandro Andrade, the 'Black Marvel', the first great black football player in the history of Uruguayan football. There is no question that football integrates and brings together. It is also a way to climb the social ladder. A great example of this was that of Abdón Porte El Indio. Maiztegui, being a great professor and orator and devout *Bolso*, told the story while sitting at his kitchen table behind a big pile of books:

'He had won the championship with Nacional and he had won the Copa America in 1917 with Uruguay but the fateful day came when the coach told him that on Sunday he would not be in the starting line-up. Abdón could not live without playing football for Nacional. Football had taught him to live in society, to dress properly, to have a bath, to get a job, and to get a girlfriend. Thus it was that on 5 March 1918, in the Gran Parque Central, the Nacional stadium, he shot himself in the head. They found him the next day with the gun still in his hand.'

This was in the 1920s, the years of success for Uruguayan football.

Mario Romano explained as he ambled through the halls to the Football Museum at the heart of the Centenary

Stadium: 'There was no particular reason behind the Uruguayan success at the start of the twentieth century.'

The manager pointed out the shirts, balls, trophies, the boots of José Vidal, number 5 for the national team of 1924 and the large photo of Andrade. He stopped to explain and provide some detail about the national trophies. Then he picked up from where he had stopped a few moments before: 'I believe it has a lot to do with the Rio de la Plata situation, with the economic power of Uruguay and Argentina, economic powerhouses at that time. They had not suffered the fallout of the First World War which had ravaged Europe. On the contrary, they saw a net increase in exports, capital investment and currency exchange. Uruguay was going through a period of growth, commercial and industrial expansion; it had a stable political regime with the state providing an advanced social welfare system and policies were in place to promote physical education which opened up the sports fields to the whole country. It was [Uruguay's] football in particular which made its mark on the Old Continent. Football had come to conquer the world and conquer it did. In Paris in 1924, Uruguay won the Olympic tournament beating Switzerland 3-0 and amazing the fans.'

Henri de Montherlant, a French novelist and playwright, wrote: 'A revelation! This is true football. The one we knew, which we played, compared to this it is just a school pastime.'

Maiztegui added: 'Uruguay was a small country which did not stand out on the world map; it made a name for itself in Europe not for its literary culture inspired by the French, not for its musical culture with strong Italian influences but for its footballers.'

It was in Paris at the Colombes stadium that the legend of *garra charrúa* (Charruan tenacity) started to embed itself in the public consciousness. The organisers did not know how to identify the players from Uruguay and so requested that a Frenchman dressed in traditional Uruguayan clothing stood in front of the Uruguayan cohort. The Uruguayan players were shocked. Their parents and grandparents came from Europe and the players did not know anything about the Indios and Aborigines who had lived in the East Strip. The last Indios, the indigenous people of Uruguay, were killed in 1831 in the *matanza de Salsipuedes* (the massacre of Salsipuedes) by Jose Fructuoso Rivera y Toscana, the first Constitutional President of Uruguay. Those that survived and were imprisoned ended up being turned into slaves in Montevideo or sent to Paris and exhibited like a circus attraction. Thanks to romantic poets like Juan Zorrilla de San Martín, the legend of the brave and fearless warrior who fought to the death against any enemy in his way lives on. *Garra charrúa* was a divine gift that enabled a warrior to give that little bit extra when the enemy least expected it.

This battle quality was transposed on to the game of football and the Uruguayan 'warriors' of football. It became the benchmark for the national team.

At the 1928 Olympics in Amsterdam, Uruguay won a second gold medal, beating their eternal rivals Argentina in the final by drawing the first leg and winning the second. At the 1929 congress in Barcelona, FIFA decided to award the organisation of the first World Cup to Uruguay: a rich country which had not suffered the 1929 Wall Street crash and the Great Depression. It was experiencing what came to be known as *los años locos* ('the crazy years'). The economy was booming. The peso was worth more than the dollar. Social mobility was on the up and the middle class saw its purchasing power improve significantly. Great warehouses opened up to manage the increase in demand for consumer goods; 15,000 cars were imported in one year alone. Montevideo was transformed: new residential areas sprang up, skyscrapers reached for the sky, hospitals, schools, universities, parks and stadiums (including the Centenary stadium) burst into life.

FIFA, which knows and has always known where the real money is, chose Uruguay because it understood that its economy could take on the cost of organising a World Cup. The Uruguayan government went even further than it was asked to: it set aside 300,000 pesos to pay for the transatlantic liners to ferry the players from the other teams from Europe to Uruguay. Accommodation was all included and a daily allowance was granted to the players and staff of France, Yugoslavia, Belgium and Romania (the only four countries from the Old Continent). In six months, the *El Centenario* stadium was built. Shift workers worked non-stop to make sure it was ready on time. It is the only stadium to have been declared a FIFA Monument to Football. The stats are impressive: capacity of 90,000; cost of 1.5 million pesos. It was designed by the architect, Juan Antonio Scasso.

The torrential rains put a hold on the opening ceremony and the stadium was opened five days after the World Cup had started. It was at 2.10pm on Saturday, 30 July 1930 that the final took place: Uruguay vs Argentina. It was a replay of what had happened two years prior in Amsterdam. Héctor Castro, the divine 'El Manco' ('one-armed'), the son of Galician immigrants – a forward who had only one hand as the other had been sawn off by an electric saw when he was a kid – he scored in the 89th minute with a superb header that took the final score to 4-2. Uruguay were champions of the world.

FIFA President Jules Rimet presented Uruguay's captain José Nasazzi, 'The Terrible', with the World Cup trophy. The country was in a state of euphoria. The government made 31 July a national holiday. The Light Blues had won 'thanks to a brilliant combination of direct and aggressive football consisting of long balls (emulating the English style) and elaborate short passes to mix the rhythm of the game up', according to sociologist, Rafael Bayce, in his book, *The Evolution of the Systems of Play*. The final in the Centenary stadium was the keystone to establishing football as a mainstream sport in the Rio de la Plata.

*

It was at 4.33pm on 16 July 1950 in Rio de Janeiro that Alcides Ghiggia, the left-winger for Uruguay, silenced the Maracanã (long before Frank Sinatra and Pope Wojtyla would do the same). Two hundred thousand people who had been convinced they were going to win fell silent. Uruguay beat Brazil and took home their second World Cup. It was the worst match played at the Maracanã, the worst tragedy from Brazil's perspective. Mario Filho wrote in his editorial in the *Jornal dos Sports*: 'The city has closed its windows and gone into mourning. It was as though every Brazilian had lost his or her loved one. Or, even worse, as though every Brazilian had lost their honour and dignity.' It was a shock to the system, a 'psychological Hiroshima' as coined by the playwright, Nelson Rodríguez; an infinite sadness which led to tears, heart attacks and suicides.

Uruguay, on the other hand, was in party mode. Obdulio Varela, the Uruguayan captain, took time to soothe Brazilian spirits: he spent the night drinking and crying with the losers and later stated: '*con la Celeste en el pecto somos dobles hombres*' (with Uruguay in our hearts we are at least twice the men we normally are). The man became a legend, a symbol for victory and the *garra charrúa*.

Sixty-five years have gone by since that fateful match, but Uruguay is still talking about it. Books are written about it, films are made about those glorious 90 minutes. No one has forgotten the Maracanazo. It is used as a reference point, with mixed results. Mario Romano interpreted that World Cup from a purely sporting event perspective: 'Maracanã was a landmark in the footballing history of Uruguay; it was its greatest achievement. It proved to everyone the *garra charrúa*, the impossible could be possible and that you should never give up; it was David vs Goliath. The flip side was that only the number one spot was acceptable. When the national team came fourth in the World Cup in Switzerland, it was treated as a failure, just like the fourth place in the 1970 World Cup. It was only 60 years later that fourth place in the South African World Cup was celebrated as it should be, with vigour and joy.'

Maiztegui added: 'The problem is not in the sporting event – which is a fact – but in how it is interpreted. Or rather: we, Uruguayans, are winners whom others study, work and prepare, train and push hard but we, with our *garra charrúa*, will always beat them. Juan Alberto Schiaffino, a graceful player, a great follower of football confessed to me: "Will they never say or write that we beat Brazil because we played great football? Will they continue to say that it was the *garra* tenacity and the fact that we are cunning and macho? An idea that has done more damage than floods, for football and for our country."'

Pepe Mujica said that after the victory, Uruguayans went to sleep and in the decade that followed the decline of a once-rich nation ensued.

Maiztegui stated: 'In 1950 Europe had other things to think about than football and slowly rebuilt its industries, social fabric and workforce to gain its place on the international stage, whereas Uruguay and for the most part all of Latin America did not work out how to make the most of the favourable economic conditions and to industrialise their economies; Uruguay started to fall behind just as it did on the pitch.'

Those who rest on their laurels get bogged down and reliant on the ideas and concepts of the past, including ideas about physical fitness, tactics and strategy. A team which is stuck in a rut does not take on new ideas and concepts; it fails to evolve. From the middle of the 1950s, the influx of migrants, which for several decades had seen thousands of immigrants come to Uruguay, was reversed and among the exodus of people were the footballers. Maiztegui added: 'Examples are Schiaffino and Ghiggia who ended up at Milan and Rome in Italy; there was José Santamaria who, after the Swiss World Cup, moved to Real Madrid and in the 1980s trained with the Spanish team. Even in our darkest hour, we have exported meat and players.'

The darkest days in the history of Uruguay started on 27 June 1973 when President Juan María Bordaberry dissolved Parliament and with the support of the army set up a civic-military dictatorship which lasted until 1985. It was a dictatorship that removed all opponents, imprisoned leftist managers and trade unionists and tortured leaders such as Mujica, who was arrested for taking part in the Tupamaros Liberation Movement. He was in prison for thirteen years. Even the traditional party followers were imprisoned. Bordaberry revoked all civil liberties and rights. Maiztegui, who was forced to leave for Spain during the years of the regime, explained: 'It was a regime that made all the structural problems of the country even worse. It buried the hatchet on the country. It is only now that we are beginning to get back what we lost in that period; 50 years of being economically static and the financial crises of 2001 and 2002.'

2005 was a turning point: Frente Amplio won the elections. He won with a coalition of leftist groups. The 2009 election of President José Mujica was also a step in the right direction. There is a different feeling in the air in Uruguay: unemployment has been reduced from 40 per cent to 6.5 per cent in nine years. The middle class have got their purchasing power back. Social policies are changing the face of the country. There is still a lot to do in terms of education and health but whilst Uruguay used to be a place to get away from, now it is a place to go to. Hope has been restored and football has benefited from this. The national side came fourth in the 2011 Copa America held in Argentina. Romano explained it as follows:

'History has repeated itself once again; external conditions have affected the world of football, even if there are still structural problems. Apart from Peñarol and Nacional, the championship has few international-level teams and the quality of the teams is not great. For these reasons, international TV companies do not follow our football. In 2006, Uruguay began a coherent training programme which led to the Under-17s and Under-20s getting to the final of the World Cup for the relevant category. However, Uruguay does not have the sponsorship and budget that other Latin American teams have, such as Brazil and Argentina, and nowhere near those of Italy and England. The biggest difference between Uruguayan football and football in the rest of the world is structural: there are simply too few structures in place to develop and train youngsters and there are no policies to change this. And yet, incredibly, what with the number of young aspiring players and a diet rich in meat and dairy, we continue to produce strong players who can easily adapt to any championship. Footballers like Luis Suárez are a reason to be proud to be Uruguayan.'

Chapter 2

Thermal baths, oranges and baby football

Ms Gladys was 85 years old but she did not look it. Wearing a light blue cardigan, necklace with matching earrings, and owlish glasses, she strolled out of a store with some shopping. She crossed the road and politely welcomed in the visitors. She opened the gate to her house and a fluffy black cat perched on the garden wall like a garden gnome, keeping a watchful eye on the world passing by. Through a long corridor and into the kitchen, full of memories. Gladys talked about her life: two husbands who died too young, children she never had; and she talked about her neighbours, the Suárez Diaz family. 'They lived just next door', Gladys explained. 'Yes, just over there.' It was a prefabricated house with a corrugated iron roof and brown walls with a green patch out front on the crossroads between Calle 6 de abril and Grito de Ascencio. Gladys's memory was spot on. She recalled Luis Suárez well: 'He played football in front of his house with his brothers. He never stopped for a minute. I saw him come and go on his way to school no. 64 in Salto.'

Salto is in the north-east of Uruguay, 498 kilometres from the capital. It is six hours by bus from the Tres Cruces terminal in Montevideo; 20 minutes from Concordia Entre Rios in Argentina. There are 104,000 inhabitants according to the latest census. It is the city with the second highest population in the Eastern Republic of Uruguay, after Montevideo. Salto, capital of the homonymous Province, takes its name from two waterfalls in the area, Salto Grande and Salto Chico. It is famous for the wonderful aroma of the juicy oranges which grow there. They are the best in the whole of South America, according to locals. It is also known for the thermal baths of Arapey and Damyán. It is not by chance that the first question asked of visitors when they arrive in Salto is 'Have you been to the thermal baths?' You cannot miss them. They rejuvenate you and you feel like a new person.

Arapey and Damyán are thermal baths with waters which have medicinal and healing properties to revitalise visitors and treat any aches and pains. The thermal waters were discovered by workers drilling for oil in the 1940s and 1950s. Today, during holy week, known to lay people as 'tourist week', adults and children alike come to visit the thermal baths. Salto is a city which lives off agriculture: citrus fruits; grapes used to make Tannat, a wine of national importance. Blueberries have also started being grown recently. Tourism and husbandry have been around for some time. Local historians say that Salto was founded on 8 November 1756 by José Joaquin de Viana, the Spanish governor of the Eastern Strip. Whilst travelling to meet Marqués de Valdelirios, the monarch's representative in outlining the boundaries, and his Portuguese counterpart, Viana stopped off in the area for a few months and built the first settlement which was made up of a few shacks for the troupes and warehouses for the cargo. Today life in Salto flows from east to west along the Calle Uruguay, the road that cuts across the centre to end up in the park which is the doorway to Rio Uruguay. There, amidst the poles, large birds hunt for insects and the white façade of the regional government building is reflected in the water. Clothes shops, bookshops, speakers pumping music in front of the shops, restaurants, bureaux de change, banks, bars, slow crawling traffic between the coloured houses. As you walk to the river, on the right there is Calle Joaquín Suárez and here, at number 39, you can see one of the most incredible monuments of Salto: the Larrañaga Theatre. It is a neo-classical building with large white pillars, blue doors, red velvet everywhere, golden frescoes and crystal lampshades: a jewel set between crumbling houses. It was an English engineer, Robert Alfred Wilkinson from Ferrocarril Noroeste, who designed it. It was opened on 6 October 1882 to a grand performance of *La Hija Unica* by the Italian drama company of Oreste Cartocci, interpreted by Gustavo Salvini.

That wonderful soirée was the first of a number of outstanding shows with artists such as Luisa Tetrazzini, Teresa Mariani and Leopoldo Fregoli putting on performances there. After years of neglect and various urban myths about the place being haunted, in 2009 it was restored to its former glory and the museum now has various shows, operas, concerts and plays which honour the legacy of the theatre. In 1912, suite number 32 of the Hotel Concordia was home to Carlos Gardel after one of his performances.

Salto's past is set in history via a futurist monolith dedicated to Casa di Quiroga. The 'hero of two worlds' lived here between 1845 and 1846 and took part in the battles of Itapebi and San Antonio in the Uruguayan Civil War. Casa di Quiroga, aka the Horacio Quiroga Mausoleum, Museum and Cultural Centre, is an ancient building in Avenida General Viera. At one time this was a holiday home. Nowadays it hosts an exhibition of various objects and the urn containing the ashes of Horacio Quiroga, narrator and playwright, modern poet and short story writer, who wrote about the Latin American world. Many have compared him to Edgar Allan Poe, author of 'The Mask of the Red Death', who Quiroga considered a master of his art. A dramatic life marked by death, hunting accidents and suicide. His tales, 'Stories of Love, Madness and Death', 'The Wild' and 'The Beheaded Chicken' are obligatory reading for school pupils in Salto.

Today the famous men of the city are not the same as the ones of old. Two massive Intendencia de Salto advertising boards hang over the main street: huge images of Edinson Cavani and Luis Suárez wearing the light blue shirt. The images are merged with blurred images of carnival dancers, the other main attraction in Salto. The carnival is a week of parades where *candombe*, *batucada* and samba merge with African and European rhythms. The drums boom and the carnival queens parade along as though they were in Rio de Janeiro.

It is not just the local council using the image of the footballers. At the crossroads between Sarandi and Calle Uruguay, Suárez's beaming smile reminds passers-by that 'Winning is easy'. Or at least that is what the Barcelona number 9 is saying in order to promote Cablevision, a local cable TV company.

Luis Alberto Suárez Diaz's first house is about twenty blocks from the centre of town. It was in this ramshackle house located on top of a hill in Barrio El Cerro that the star lived the first years of his life. Suárez was born on 24 January 1987 in Salto's hospital. He was the fourth son of Sandra and Rodolfo. Before him came Paolo, Giovanna and Leticia and after him came Maximiliano and Diego. A healthy kid who, unlike his brothers and sisters, did not even get the dreaded chickenpox. However, at two years old, he gave his parents a fright when he became ill with appendicitis and then two days after the operation he got peritonitis. The pain was unbearable and the little Suárez could not even stand up. It was simply an unforeseen complication after a routine operation. The doctors had to re-open the wound and sort it out. Slowly but surely, the intestinal infection healed and Suárez got better.

He was a scrawny kid with a full head of dark hair; his friends and family gave him the nickname, '*Cabeza*' or '*Cabezón*' ('Big Head').

Lila Píriz, Luis's grandmother on his father's side, was waiting in the patio at the house in Calle Ozimane. She waited a moment before opening the gate. She apologised for not being able to invite the visitor into the dining room. There were people sleeping there. The next day there was going to be a big party for the 60-year anniversary of her marriage to Atasildo Suárez. He was 21 years old and she fifteen when they got married. They had six children, who in turn gave them 23 grandchildren and 23 great-grandchildren. Many of them had come over from Montevideo to celebrate. Two women were in the kitchen starting the preparations: huge loaves of bread were being stacked in a pile. Outside on the patio, where a green parrot was squawking in its cage, Lila warned the visitors not to go near him: 'He will bite your hand off if you put your finger anywhere near the cage'. Atasildo, dark eyed and with a cap on his head, was resting on a deckchair. In the background, the fields and green landscape of Salto stretched into the distance. Lila talked about her grandson, 'El Cheo' as she called him: 'He was a good kid and football was everything for him. He played from dawn till dusk. He was always polite with everyone. It's been several years since he upped and left, first for Montevideo and then to Europe.' Luis could not make the 60th wedding anniversary celebrations. Atasildo continued: 'But for us, knowing what he has achieved and where he has got to makes us very proud.' The grandparents made no further comments on the subject.

Many have come from all over – England, Japan, you name it – to get the lowdown on the Suárez family. Many a rumour has been spread in Salto about this family.

The rumours started in the first months of 2014 when a local newspaper ran a story that María Josefa Reyes la Pelusa, 65 years old, Luis' grandmother on his mother's side, had come back to Salto as she was not well and she did not have a house to live in. The papers ran amok, smelling the blood of a scandal which they could exploit to sell papers. There were accusations of her son asking the local council to build her a house; snipes about Luis not digging into his pockets to help out his poorly grandma; rumours that Luis was not even aware of the situation or that he was and that he had sent money. The upshot was that it was a family issue which was no business of anyone else but the family.

Luis's father Rodolfo Suárez was in the military, just like his own father had been: *Batallón de Infantería 7 Ituzaingó* (Ituzaingó 7th battalion), an institution which was 100 years old in 2010. Pepe Mujica paid homage to the institution as a sign of *rapprochement* between the leftist government and the armed forces. General Artigas' barracks, where the Ituzaingó 7th battalion and the 3rd Infantry Brigade are based, is a few hundred metres from Lila Píriz and Atasildo's home. The barracks are made up of a green square with a few silos fenced off with turrets where armed soldiers stand on watch. The signs outside the barracks read: 'Military zone. No entry'. A line of yellow cabins runs along the perimeter of the barracks. These are the homes of the soldiers' families. It is here at number 1120 that the Suárez Díaz family moved to. Few remember the little Luis Suárez. Every four years the yellow cabins are homes to different families. And yet 'El Pistolero' ('The Shooter', as he would come to be known) started playing seriously when he lived here, playing at the military base's club. It was here in 1964 that the military base set up Club Deportivo Artigas, the 'soldiers' club', as it was known. Various military personnel played for the team. Miguel, intent on rebuilding the roof of the club headquarters, explained: 'During the period of military dictatorship there was plenty of money to splash on the club and for equipment and pitches, something which few other clubs could afford at that time.' The *milicos* (military men) have always been fans of football. There are many in Salto who remember the siren of the Battalion sounding when Uruguay beat Korea in the 2010 World Cup. The siren went on for a long time. The same thing happened when Uruguay beat Brazil in Maracanã in 1950 and won their second World Cup.

Rodolfo Suárez was a good defender who played on the right. It was not easy getting past him. Some, like José, who had played against Deportivo Artigas or against Salto, remembered 'El Quito' Suárez as a player who went in hard, never stopped talking on the pitch and got angry with the opponents; a bit of a 'dirty player', all things considered. A hard nut who could be quick-witted and crafty depending on the situation: a quality which Luis seems to have inherited.

Nowadays Deportivo Artigas, '*El Club de Familia*', is a club in its own right. There are military personnel, trade unionists and workers all playing alongside each other. The club offers various sporting activities, from athletics to swimming, rugby to hockey. At the crossroads between Calle Apollon de Mirbeck and Avenida Feliciano Viera, a few hundred metres from the barracks, Deportivo Artigas has built its impressive sports complex. There is a bust of José Gervasio Artigas, the founding father of the nation, on the grass square in front of the complex. There is the social centre which looks like a ranch from the countryside, with a large hall for parties and a little office with cups, medals and pennants, an impressive statue of the Madonna and a sign that reads: 'Football isn't easy, it is ... simple'. Once inside, there is the obligatory *asado* (barbecue) to cook the food on, three football pitches (one artificial grass pitch for kids and two grass pitches with stands. One of these is the official pitch and can take up to 800 spectators). There are changing rooms, a swimming pool and stalls for hippotherapy. The sports complex was opened in 2010 thanks to the financial contribution of the members and $400,000 from the *Oficina de Cooperación de Defensa* (Defence Cooperation Office) of the United States government and various national institutions. In the first few years of the 1990s, there was nothing here. The matches and the training sessions were held on the pitch at the military base. It was a meeting place for everyone in the area. In the afternoon, kids on their way home from school would drop their bags off at home before heading over to the base to play or to watch their dads training. It was a crime to miss a single day. If the pitches were full, play carried on makeshift pitches or in the streets of El Cerro which, even today, are still not tarmacked. Barefoot with a makeshift football. Luis Suárez started exactly like this. At four or five years old, he went with his older brother Paolo (then aged eleven) and gave the older boys a run for their money. Matches would go on for hours. Only dinner would interrupt play. Even at home, kids would find a way to carry on playing, heading and playing keepy-up. Luis once broke his parents' bed. Anywhere was fair game: at home, in the street and on the dusty patches of land. There was even baby football.

Don Alfredito Honsi, a man with a flush of white hair and a minute physique, was the founding father of football for kids in Salto. He was the one who brought baby football to the city. In the 1960s, he founded the *Liga de Baby Fútbol* (Baby Football League) of Ceibal. A decade later, he founded the *Liga Salteña de Baby* (Saltena Baby League) and in 1987 a baby world cup. It was a competition for kids from the age of four to six ('pre-baby' and 'baby') which took place every December and January during the school holidays. Thirty-five teams, four to five matches of fifteen-minute halves starting at 7.00 every evening. Large crowds paid five pesos each to watch the matches. The money was used to buy the 400 medals, one for each kid taking part, and the prizes (books, pencils, rubbers, pencil cases, crayons). The tournament was held in the patio of the Recreational Centre of East Salto (CRES, or East Zone) at no. 1739 of Calle 19 de abril. It was a long white building in front of Plaza de los Deportes.

The patio is overrun with plants and trees nowadays. The goals are in a bad way. The nets are no longer there and two dogs keep guard, snoozing in the shade.

Alfredo Honsi, Don Alfredino's son, has set up a community radio station, Impactos FM, in the grounds. Alfredo explained that the local council was meant to be helping out to restore the patio, the home to baby football, balls, shows and fêtes. Honsi provided an insight into what the future held: 'They are going to do a documentary, the people from Montevideo, the reason being that Luis Suárez and Edinson Cavani played here. One played for Deportivo Artigas, the other for Nacional de Salto. The player who scored the most goals usually ended up in the ice-cream parlour ten metres down the road. The best prize of all was a large Cornetto.'

El Cabeza was trained by his uncle, Sergio 'El Chango' Suárez. He was the one who taught him how to kick a ball at four years of age, when Luis was the club mascot. Even El Chango lived in a humble low-level house in Barrio El Cerro. Despite the rundown look of the area, people took pride in their surroundings. At the door of the house, several kids came running to answer it. The youngest kid was dressed in a Spider-man costume and stared bemusedly at the visitor. The kid opened the door and did the honours. The lady of the house said that her husband was at work and would be back at midday for lunch. El Chango was on time. He rolled up on his motorbike and, before parking, he gave his son a quick blast around the block. El Chango sat down in the dining room in his blue work overalls. He started to explain. The timbre of his voice was soft and quiet. He started off by talking about his work as a carpenter and his past as a footballer for Deportivo, Phoenix and Colombia: these were all amateur clubs which no longer exist.

There are no professional clubs in Salto but there are five amateur leagues: Liga Salteña, Liga Colonias agrarias, Liga fútbol comercial, Liga senior (over-35s), Liga master (over-45s). And that is not including the Selección Salteña or baby football. These leagues have produced a number of great footballers from Alexander Medina to Gonzalo de Los Santos, from Bruno Fornaroli to Cavani, all of whom left, going first to the Uruguayan capital and then variously to Argentina, Chile and Europe. But let us get back to Luis: what was he like?

'He was just like he is now. Football was everything to him. He woke up with a football and went to bed with one. He played in the street just like them', he points to the kids outside, who have abandoned their computer games and the TV to practise football skills. Sergio continued: 'At first Luis was a bit awkward with the ball but he committed to every ball. He did not leave any move unfinished. He wanted to win. He wanted to score, he wanted to be the goalscorer, whatever it took. Exactly as he does now.'

'Was the winner of the 2014 Golden Shoe really awkward with the ball?'

Sergio replied without hesitating: 'He was better in defence, so much so that when we played against tough opponents, I put him in goal. He did not like that but he did his best. He saved the day on many occasions.'

It was odd to think of Luis Suárez playing in goal. Sergio

got up from the sofa and disappeared into the bowels of the house for a moment. He came back a few minutes later with a plastic bag. The writing on the bag read 'Mafalda', the lead character of a comic strip illustrated by Quino. The bag contained memories of times gone by.

With his silver hair, rounded spectacles and a beaming smile across his face, Sergio leant over the table and pulled out a pile of Polaroids. There was baby Deportivo Artigas with Luis in front of goal; there were photos of the CRES patio, kids with arms folded and serious expressions on their faces staring into the lens – just like adult players do before a big match. The strip was red with white and blue stripes and light blue shorts. Sergio commented: 'The strip is pretty much the same as that of Independiente Argentino'.

But where was Luis? It was hard to recognise him. El Chango pointed to him with his index finger: a darkly scruffy-haired kid with a cheeky smile was staring up. Sergio added: 'You should recognise him here.' The kids were lined up in order of height at the edge of the tufty grass pitch. Sergio too was in the picture, considerably younger and with dark brown hair. He was lining them up. Luis was third along with shorts that were too big for him, holding back a smile.

Another picture of Luis in goal. Luis had a monk haircut like the Beatles in the 1960s. His strip was orange; he was standing with his hands behind his back on the second row, right next to his uncle who was trying to get a kid in front of him to stop fidgeting. El Chango handed across another photo, one of his own son playing for Nacional. He continued: 'In our family, we all play football. My son tried for the youth team at Nacional but he did not make it.' Yet another family photo. This time Luis and his brother Maxi, with Braian Rodríguez of Salto fame. Sergio explained: 'Braian plays in Brazil now'.

Though Sergio's wife said there was plenty of time despite there being guests, it was time for lunch and time to leave.

But first, one more thing: 'What is the best memory from the years gone by?'

Sergio laughed and replied: 'The best thing I recall is when, in the middle of a match, Luis raised his hand and asked the referee to stop play so he could go to the toilet. Another one is when he was five years old. He was playing when he saw his brother, Paolo, in the crowd, eating a piping hot pizza. Luis kicked the ball into touch and ran to Paolo to get a slice. Paolo told him to get back on the pitch but Luis was having none of it. Luis was screaming, he wanted the pizza. Typical boyish antics. Luis was a good kid, just like he is now.'

One final question: 'Luis has often mentioned that you taught him to touch the *pelota* [ball]. What did you teach him?' Sergio answered: 'I did not teach him anything. He already had the basics. What he has achieved is all down to him.'

Braian Rodríguez paints a different picture. The 29-year-old Grêmio forward, who grew up playing for baby Deportivo Artigas and then Cerro, Peñarol and in Argentina, Chile and Spain, has not forgotten El Chango's advice: 'He taught us to love football and to live it with passion. This was important advice which, as a kid, stays with you for the rest of your life. He taught us how to move on the pitch and caress the ball; he explained how to kick, tackle, free yourself from markers and finish off a move; he taught us that football is a team game and that there is no point playing for yourself, and that passing is key. All of these things are counterintuitive when you are a kid. He was a great teacher. Without his help, we may not have made it to where we are today'.

At the end of training, before grabbing a shower, Braian reminisced over the first few years when he started playing football: 'They were happy times, we had a lot of fun. We learnt a whole load of things. When December came around and we knew the dates of the baby World Cup, we were feverish with excitement. Everyone wanted to win the title, to be the best team and to be the top goalscorer. It was a party.' Braian noted, from one striker to another: 'My father was in the army, just like Quito Suárez. He played in goal for Deportivo Artigas. I grew up with Luis in the pre-baby and baby matches. As a goalie he was pretty good. On the pitch he was fast, decisive, just like his dad, able to skim past two or three opponents.

'Baby Deportivo was a team which was virtually unbeaten. Nobody wanted to play against us. When he was seven, Luis left for Montevideo with his family and sometime later I also moved there to play for Cerro. This is the destiny for many Salto players who, thanks to baby football, the matches on makeshift pitches and street matches, dream of playing in the big leagues for Montevideo, Nacional or Peñarol as a launchpad to Europe or elsewhere abroad.'

It was 1994 when Rodolfo Suárez asked to be transferred to Montevideo. Luis did not want to leave Salto. No one could convince him it was a good idea – so much so that he stayed with his grandmother for a month before joining up with his family. And then that was it. He left for the capital and would only return to Salto on the odd occasion. Unlike Cavani, who stayed in Salto until he was sixteen and when he can he goes back to go fishing in Río Uruguay, chill out with friends and family and recharge his batteries, Luis did not go back, despite the request of the local council and his first school. Montevideo was where his family and friends were, his father, his brothers. This is why some say he is not really a 'salteño'. It is the classic story of those who leave a place early in their lives. It was a way of turning a page in his life.

Chapter 3

The long walk south

From the north to the south, from the provinces to the capital in search of a job, following a dream, utopia or simply a chance to make things happen. From the interior of Uruguay to Montevideo is a journey many Uruguayans make, including the Suárez Diaz family.

They loaded all their stuff on a lorry and two days later Suárez's mother Sandra and her children climbed on the bus which would take them across pastures where cows grazed and onwards towards the city where Rodolfo was waiting for them. Luis came into contact with the city which is now home to 1.4 million people – around 40 per cent of the population. He saw the Rio de La Plata: enormous, majestic, endless, with its ochre-coloured waters cut up by container ships heading in and out of the port. The estuary runs alongside the entire city. It rumbles alongside the Rambla, it brings the various quarters of the city together, it passes car parks, beaches, skyscrapers overlooking the water and comes near to the Avenida 18 de Julio, the busiest commercial street of the city, which starts at Plaza Independencia, the meeting point of the old and new city. It was here in 1928 that Mario Palanti, an Italian architect, helped realise the highest building in all of Latin America: the Salvo Building. It was and is a folly, an icon of Montevideo, appearing on all the postcards of the city. A famous photo from 1934 shows the German airship Graf Zeppelin passing over the top of the building.

The old city: fantastic buildings from the era in Uruguay's history when it was the Switzerland of South America; today they are crumbling.

Finally the estuary reaches the port which, after several years of little activity, is starting to come to life again (albeit Buenos Aires still has the upper hand). A few metres away is the market, built by British engineers using iron imported from the Liverpool Union Foundry. From the entrance to the market, which is now a permanent *asado*, you can see the huge building which is home to the general headquarters of Customs and the Navy General Command offices. This striking building would not look out of place in Gotham City.

The Suárez Diaz family moved to La Blanqueada, on the crossroads between Duvimioso Terra and Nicaragua, ten minutes from the centre by car. It is a quarter where people are mad about football. Between the low-level houses of Blanqueada, there is the Gran Parque Central stadium, where on 13 July 1930, in front of 19,000 fans, the first match of the first World Cup was played: USA vs Belgium – final score 3-0. The Parque Central is home to Nacional, the team Luis and his brothers follow passionately.

Leaving football to one side, the move from Salto to Montevideo, from the hinterland to the big city, was not without its complications for the kids of the Suárez family. They had to leave all their grandparents, uncles, aunts, relatives and childhood friends behind. They were used to playing on the streets from morning to night. In Blanqueada this was not possible.

It was not just the metropolis with its lights, noises, traffic, pollution or immense estuary that surprised them but more the reaction of the people. The Montevideans made fun of their accent, of how they said 'dad' and 'mum', of how they dressed, of their old outdated shoes, of the fact that they were country bumpkins and of the fact that at break time the Suárez kids had to make do with a bit of bread and marmalade whereas the local kids could buy a nice cake or some fried food.

Luis Suárez has admitted on several occasions that, 'we were a lower class family and also a numerous family and so we could not afford certain treats. I never asked my parents to buy me the pair of football boots which I was so longing for. My parents did all they could and I am very grateful to them but they could not provide for us as they wanted to, just the bare minimum.'

Rodolfo, Suárez' father, left the army and found a job in a biscuit factory, El Trigal; Sandra was a cleaner at Tres Cruces, the city's major bus terminal. Luis went to school number 171, as did his brothers, between Nicaragua and Cufré. Luis liked maths and got on with his homework at home. Who knows – if he hadn't been a footballer maybe he could have been a good accountant. And yet the first few months were difficult because Luis did not understand why he needed to study multiplication tables, seeing as he did not need them to score goals. Luis loved football more than anything else.

His first idols and role models were in his family: his father and his brother, Paolo, played too. Paolo plays for Club Atlético Basáñez in the Uruguayan Second Amateur Division. Luis copied movements and gestures from Paolo and his brother patiently taught him the tricks of the trade. His next idol was Ronaldo, 'O' Fenómeno', then Fernando Cavenaghi of River Plate and then Gabriel Batitusta, the Argentinian who played for Fiorentina, Roma and Inter. Batitusta was an example of what it meant to be a modern forward. Luis studied his idols and played with his younger (by one year) brother, Maximiliano, for Urreta FC, a baby football club in Blanqueada at the crossroads between Arrieta and Pedro Vidal. Sandra took Luis there at seven years old. She was looking for a club to let her boys play. Everyone spoke highly of Urreta, a team which had pitches near Canal 5 and which had taught generations of kids the rules of the game.

Ricardo Artigas, club secretary for the last five years, explains the history of the club: 'Urreta FC was founded in 1958 by Adolfo Bañales and his wife Blanca Gómez. This couple decided to put together a team so that the kids in the area could have fun and play together. It was no easy task. They had to convince the kids to meet, get permission from parents and fight with the local public authorities to get a permit to build a pitch in the square where today the club's headquarters are located. In those early days, the Bañaleses' home was the registered office of the club, the changing rooms and referees' room and the hostel for those kids who came from afar and had to sleep over. The opening was riddled with all kinds of problems but in the end the Bañaleses got there and opened the club. They even managed to find a sponsor: the Urreta drinks factory which, at that time, was just opposite the club. Today there is the pasta factory Las Acacias. Urreta paid for the first shirts and used the factory's name for the name of the club.'

When Luis Suárez turned up for a trial with the club, the club had already established itself and had won many titles and trophies. They took a look at Luis running with the ball and decided he could stay with the club. A few days later, 'El Salta' or 'El Salteño' ('the one from Salto' or 'the little one from Salto'), as he was known to the coaches and his friends, was put on the bench for a match at Lagomar, a residential area on the coast about 30 minutes from the centre of the city. No one had seen him play at that point; they did not know him well so it was better to err on the side of caution. At the end of the first half, Urreta was losing 2-0. The coach decided it was time to give the new boy a shot. Luis put on his checked orange shirt, similar to the Dutch one of Marco van Basten and Ruud Gullit in the 1988 European Championship, and headed on to the pitch sporting the number 14 on his back. Luis turned the game around. Three goals in true opportunist style. Urreta won the match and 'El Salta' gained the trust of his coach.

While trawling through the archives one day, Artigas found the teamsheet of the baby football team of 87. He read it out loud to me: 'Federico Picardo, Cesar Mareco, Leonardo Quintana, Maximiliano Pérez, Mateo Espasandin, Martin Píriz, Luis Suárez, Camilo Correa, Jorge Bottias, Ignacio Betancourt, Sebastián Canabe, Marcelo García, Emiliano Prado, Ramiro Silveira.'

The secretary had managed to get hold of the list of the titles won, including the *La Liga Prado* and the *Metropolitano Circuito 1* and *2*; there were even photos of the matches and the celebrations afterwards, with a young Suárez beaming and holding a cup in his hand. Artigas said: 'There is someone who knows a lot more than I do, though: Florean Neira, his first coach.'

Neira had just come back from his afternoon walk, after having observed the young kids playing football in the park nearby. Neira, who is in his eighties now, before even sitting down for dinner, started to tell his story:

'I have always loved teaching *botijas* (kids) the fundamentals of the game, how to control the ball, play with your head held high, pass the ball and not try to win the game on your own. I always wanted them to progress and make a career for themselves. As a coach, I was with Club Deportivo Oriental teaching baby football for seventeen years. From that club came the likes of Carusini, Filomeno, Dario Pereira Vicar, Carmagna. These were players who raced up and down the pitch. Thanks to the help of a friend I ended up at Urreta. Suárez, 'El Salteño', was one of my players. He was an extra-ordinary kid, with a strong personality; he was afraid of no one and sometimes argued with the other team's players. He liked chips which my wife made, Luz Divina; he came to eat at my house quite often. He was a great striker and scored lots of goals. He was a key player for us.'

The memories of the old coach were confirmed by a local newspaper article from 6 September 1996 which Luis has kept. In the Minisport section, Gustavo Acevedo and Magdalena Horta told the story of three matches against the Club Las Flores from 87, 88 and 89. This was the text of the article:

'In the third match of the day, Urreta won 3-2 in the 87 category. The first goal was scored by Luis Suárez. A few minutes later, the team in orange increased their lead with a free-kick from Martín Píriz. It looked like that was it for the first half but Flores pulled two goals back with goals from Marcio Núñez and Fernando Reyas. 2-2 at half time. The second half was a feisty affair with both sides going at it hammer and tongs. Just in the nick of time in the last few minutes, Luis Suárez scored the winning goal for the home team. Urreta was able to rely on Luis Suárez, a complete goalscorer and Martín Píriz who, despite his age, is already a free-kick specialist. These two players were fundamental for Urreta's victory today in a very intense match.'

Luis' name was in the papers. His lucky charm had worked. This was a 1 peso coin which he had found on the street before the match. Not knowing where to put it, he slotted it in his sock. He scored a hat-trick and from then on he never let it go. The on-pitch events at Urreta were going well for Luis. The same could not be said for his family life. Maximiliano would confess to *So Foot*, a French magazine, several years later: 'My dad was an alcoholic. He would go to the stadium when we were playing and shout and talk randomly to people. It was embarrassing. It was the same at home. Arguing was constant between my mum and my dad.'

In 1996, when Maxi was eight and Luis nine, Rodolfo and Sandra got divorced. The two brothers were too young to understand and take sides. The only thing that was certain was that the family situation was hard to deal with – it was a wound which would not heal. Rodolfo had left his job at the biscuit factory and moved to Carrasco in another part of the city, where he had found a job as a porter in a building in front of Club Biguá of Villa Biarritz. His sons saw him rarely but they did keep in touch (as Luis would confess years later). At that time, things were tough. There were no state rations available. Sandra, who would remarry a few years later, a construction worker with whom she would have another child, was forced to take on more work to feed her kids. She started cleaning in a hospital. The money was still not enough. Things were so bad that, as Maxi recalled: 'We lived in a single room of 5 × 3 metres. For months on end, we ate the same thing: sausages and rice. They were cheap.'

Luis, Maxi and Diego, the youngest in the family, spent most of their time alone. They were looked after by María Josefa, their grandmother on their mum's side. María Josefa moved to Montevideo to help out and to work at the Tres Cruces. Just like all kids that age, the brothers fell out a lot but they also looked out for one another when someone at school or on the street had it in for them. Luis, the oldest of the three brothers, took on the father role. They would walk or take the bus to training and Luis would wait for the other brothers after training to take them home. He was forced to grow up very quickly both on and off the pitch. His on-pitch development was so quick, in fact, that at age eleven, Nacional started to show interest in him.

Florean Neira recalled: 'We would go and train at the Gran Parque Central. A scout from *Los Bolsos* (Nacional) asked me who the young boy was. He asked me to send him to Nacional. I said no problem. I have never got in the way of a kid progressing in his career. And this time was no exception. I approved his transfer.'

This was how Neira remembered it but who knows if that was how things actually went. Especially considering that Rodolfo, Luis's father, was contacted by Danubio, another Montevideo club, regarding a potential transfer and they even offered Rodolfo money for Luis to go to their team. But Luis' dream from when he was eight years old was to wear the Nacional shirt and win the title wearing that same shirt.

In 1998, after the father of Urreta teammate Martín Píriz called him while he was on holiday for a baby football trial at Nacional, the dream became reality.

Chapter 4
A lot of heart

Luis was twelve when he started training with the youth team at Nacional. The coaches were not unanimous in their opinion on the young Suárez. Some said he was clumsy with the ball at his feet, awkward, he did not have the technical skills to be playing for one of the greatest Uruguayan clubs. Maxi, his brother, on the other hand, knew what he was doing; he had great touch with his feet, so much so that the coaches promoted him to the next category way ahead of time. But there were those, like Wilson Píriz, who believed in Luis. Wilson could see the true goalscoring colours behind the awkwardness. Wilson, the ex-*delegado* (representative) of the Nacional youth teams turned sports agent, stated: 'He had the virtues, good luck, instinct, innate ability, flukiness, call it what you will; the ball always ended up at his feet and somehow he put it in the back of the net – even blindfolded.' Basically the long and short of it was that at thirteen Luis was hired by Nacional but due to the regulations he could not sign on before then.

He was a good kid, humble, shy, reserved but responsible. Luis applied himself on the pitch and at school. He got on easily with new groups of players and schoolmates. He had plied his trade in the *Liga dell'Aufi* (the Youth Football Association League). The club adopted him, mollycoddled him and occasionally gave him some *pesos* so that he and his brothers could get the bus home. He would often eat in the club canteen where Yudith had become a second mother to him. He made friends with Víctor El Manteca and Martín. They became inseparable. Luis stayed over at their house on several occasions and years later when Víctor's father was down on his luck, he helped him to get another job.

El Salteño was going through a difficult time with his family but he somehow kept it together and carried on. However, suddenly out of the blue something went wrong; something changed, something triggered in his head and he went off the rails. His parents' divorce which had finally hit home? Puberty, which can make any kid go mad? Other interests outside of football: girls, social life or nightlife? Getting into bad company who smoke and drink to the early hours? There was a bit of everything, sending Luis on a downward spiral. One thing was clear. Football was no longer his main goal in life. He was in Nacional's seventh team (Under-14s) but on the bench. The reason? Easy: his performances were so poor that at the end of the season he had only scored eight goals. He had no desire to train and when he did train he did it begrudgingly; he ate all the sorts of things a player should not eat, like pizza, hot dogs and Coke. He behaved like he had never behaved before. On the bus to matches, he would shout and gesture and pour water on passers-by; practical jokes which kids play but which did not go down well with the managers of the club. He was on his way out; those that mattered at Nacional wanted him out. He could find another place to play and mess around. He did not have the stature and the determination to wear the Nacional shirt. This was what many at the club thought.

Luckily Wilson Píriz and José Luis Espósito, *delegado* (representative) at that time but now driving buses for a living, intervened. These were two key figures at Nacional at that time. Luis has acknowledged that these two individuals saved him from his fall from grace. Why were they so important?

Píriz commented on the episode as follows: 'I was one of the people who tried to put him back on the straight and narrow, to guide him back to where he should be when everyone else at Nacional was down on him and the club eschewed him. I just added that extra grain of sand, nothing more. I defended him and someone listened to me. This meant that Luis could carry on with the club.'

Píriz went further than just speaking to the managers of the club and convincing them after long negotiations on Luis' behalf; he spoke to the player himself to make him understand the importance of what was going on: 'I told him that if he did not behave as he was meant to behave, in the way I told him and on his best behaviour, he had to go. It was time to sort his life out both from a sports perspective and a personal life perspective; he had to work hard to work through the ranks and make it as a professional. He got the gist of what I told him and made the most of that second chance; today he is one of the best in the world.'

But what was going on with the fourteen-year-old Suárez?

Píriz commented: 'At that age, his family life had affected him deeply and Luis was no different to the other kids. Just like any teenager he liked going to parties, hanging out with friends, going to birthday parties etc. He did not want to miss out on those things. He came to training but, with only a few hours' sleep under his belt, he was not firing on all cylinders. That life affected his football. Luis was intelligent enough to realise that he could make it. He listened to the best people around him, took on board their advice; he listened to Paolo, his brother, Sofia, his fiancée at the time, and now his wife. He got back on the greasy pole.'

And what advice did Wilson Píriz give to that kid who was a future champion?

'I taught him what I had learned from life: to be a good person, a sorted individual, to not rush into things, to be confident and have faith in his abilities and to train hard to meet his goals. I simply tried to make him understand what his path in life was. I too had a harsh upbringing: my mother had to bring up my sister on her own. All the problems Luis was going through, I had been through myself; I tried to communicate my experience to him. At Nacional, we supported him in everything we could; we could not be a father to him but we could do our best so that he felt supported and wanted. I have kids and Luis was like a son to me. I always believed in him. I used to bet to myself that he would make the big league because I knew what he was capable of. He was level-headed, determined and was hungry for success. He had a lot of heart. A heart so big that it has made him into the man and footballer he is today. It is his big heart, his open nature, his easy-going attitude that won the hearts and minds of his teammates, his coaches and his managers.'

With his heart on his sleeve, his grit and his goals, Luis had made it through a dark time and started to make his impression on the youth teams. The chance to establish himself again came in the Rivera Cup against San Eugenio de Artigas. Suárez started on the bench but Bruno Fornaroli, the player from Salto, now playing for Danubio, who took Suárez's place up front, got injured. Ricardo Perdomo, the coach of the sixth team (Under-15s) gave Luis his chance. Nacional won 5-1 and Luis scored four of the five goals. It was the same story the next day against Oriental; final score 5-0 and another blinder from Luis. From that moment on, no one put Luis on the bench. At the end of the season, he had scored 25 goals. In 2003, he scored 63! Suárez missed out on Rubén Sosa's record from years earlier by one goal.

Mathías Cardacio, who grew up with Luis in the youth teams at Nacional and now plays centre midfield for Defensor Sporting in Montevideo, remembered Luis as follows: 'I remember a match against Huracán de Paso de la Arena where Luis scored eleven goals. He was the top goalscorer for 87. A winning generation that one. We had a really strong team with a fantastic attack. Luis, Martín [Cauteruccio who now plays in Argentina for San Lorenzo de Almagro] and Bruno [Fornaroli] were capable of scoring 50 or more goals a season. They were so prolific that they won every category. Luis and I were like brothers; we ribbed each other constantly and shared great moments together. He was a top kid. He was always smiling and joking. We got up to all sorts of antics … There was only one thing that he could not stomach and that was losing. He also wanted to score in every game he played. When he did not score, he got really pissed off.'

There was a match for Nacional where Nacional won 3-0 against Tacuarembó but Luis did not score. He went ballistic and stormed off to the showers to cool down. He cried with rage. It was 2003 and Suárez registered with two teams at the same time: Quinta and Cuarta.

Ricardo Perdomo, aka Murmullo (a nickname he got due to his tone of voice which sounds like a whisper), explained: 'Saturday he would play for one team and Sunday the other, Sometimes he would play in three different categories in the same week. Even if he did not get the weekend off, he was happy. He never looked sad because he was missing out on things. His life was and is football. He loves the game. You can see from how he celebrates his goals. It does not matter if it is the third or the fourth, he always celebrates with the same intensity as if each one were for a great triumph.'

Perdomo was Suárez' coach from 2002 to 2005 before the eighteen-year-old Luis played for the Nacional first team on the advice of Perdomo. Ricardo is an ex-footballer for Nacional, Rayo Vallecano in Madrid, River Plate in Buenos Aires and the Chilean Union Española in Independencia. Perdomo went over 'Lucho's' childhood while sipping a cappuccino: 'What I liked about Luis was his ability to learn. In just two years, he picked up the knowledge, ability, technique and skill that other kids had not or could not. He was always learning. Each training session was a chance to learn something new for him. He set himself targets and did his utmost to make sure he reached them. It was a personal challenge to make sure he headed the ball better, kicked the ball cleaner, kicked with his weaker left foot and executed free-kicks better. The only thing which I held him up for was his impatience to head toward the goal. He was too keen to get to the goalmouth sometimes. Even before he had touched the ball to pass to his teammate, he would be running toward the other team's area. I asked him how could he expect to receive an assist, the perfect pass or lob if the lay-off was not good. Plus if you keep playing the same move, at the second or third attempt, a good defender will have worked out what you are doing and will anticipate it. We practised the lay-off a thousand times in training; that first touch, the pass, the trigger to the start of the move. Today we see the results of all that hard work.

'On the pitch, the thing that amazes you is how easily he gets to the goal. He makes a couple of odd turns and he is in front of goal ready to strike. There is no doubting his personality as well. He never gives up on a ball. With all of the kids I taught, I drove home this point: if you chase down one or two balls, you have one or two chances but if you chase down ten balls you have a greater chance of converting. I never needed to say it twice to Luis. He did it all the time. Off the pitch he was a normal guy but on the pitch he transformed. It was his way of living football: to the max, passionately and on the edge. It is this way of interpreting the game that has made him into a great player. Even if sometimes he goes too far.'

An example of this was 2002 when he was playing a decisive match for Nacional and he got a yellow card from the referee for a foul on a defender. He argued with the referee until he got so wound up he headbutted the official. This was a terrible gesture and he risked being banned for months. Luis said he did not do it on purpose and that he did not want to hurt the guy. It was an instinctive act which he just did without thinking.

Perdomo continued whilst sipping on what was now a cold cappuccino: 'He has made many mistakes because of his temper but he has understood the error of his ways. At the end of the day, in life, we all make mistakes. Some mistakes are worse than others. Luis has always played matches at 1,000mph. He wants to win so badly that sometimes he loses his head and forgets what he is doing. His reactions may seem odd, bizarre and troublesome for those who do not know him. But I know him and they are just spur-of-the-moment reactions; there is no evil or bad will behind the gestures.'

Perdomo took another sip and a drink of water: 'Whilst still paying the maximum respect to all the brilliant players from Uruguay, Luis has reached the top. He has achieved extraordinary things. If you take a step back and look at football from the outside in, you know that a player has two or three useful options when faced with a given situation and Luis always chooses the right one. He is verging on perfection.'

Chapter 5

A marvellous surprise

A conversation with Rubén Sosa

A photo from years ago showed them next to one another. Luis was wearing a white Nacional shirt, holding a trophy in his hand and grinning like a Cheshire cat. He had been awarded the top goalscorer award for the youth league. Rubén Sosa, wearing a polo neck and jeans, was helping the kid hold the silver-plated ball which he had just been handed. The sky over Montevideo was a pale blue and Luis Suárez, who was leaning his head against Sosa's shoulder, was clearly chuffed at being able to pose for a photo with one of his heroes.

It was an ordinary afternoon in a bar in Carrasco: Rubén Sosa, now with a tiny goatee, a few grey hairs and a few more pounds than when he was a pro, had taken time out to come and chat about that little kid who is now one of the best players in the world. It was not the best day for it, especially as Sosa was moving house from one side of Montevideo to the other, but he still turned up early for the appointment. The ex-pro, who has played for Danubio, Nacional, Lazio, Inter, Borussia Dortmund and Shanghai Shenhua, was happy to talk about *El Pistolero* during his time at Nacional:

'We all knew he was able to muddle through; not because he had great technique – he does not even have that now. No, he had a spirit, a winning mentality which was second to none. When he was young, with the ball at his feet, he was by no means the best in his class. He fell over, he slid too easily, when he kicked the ball he even kicked up a chunk of grass. He was a bit clumsy: he would miss an open goal and then he would score one from an impossible angle. Even when you thought it was impossible.'

When did you meet him?
'When I came back from Spain, from Logroñes. I was playing for Nacional, he was in the youth teams, then I trained him for a bit when he was promoted to the first team. I was assistant coach for the forwards. I remember I told him that he wanted to score too quickly, he was always pushing on, looking for the goal; he wanted to win and it was for this reason that he missed goals. In the first matches, he missed about twelve chances. I told him to relax and that when he scored the first goal, the rest would follow. You just need to be patient, I told him. I was convinced because he was a very fit player with a strong background and was fearless of others. He would chase down every ball. The ball would fly to the corner post and he would chase after it to see if he could save it. He would slide to try and keep it in. It was as though he was playing rugby!

'Since then he has improved massively. His initial progress with Nacional was complicated. We would win but because Luis was transfixed with this desire to win, he would miss easy chances and the crowd would boo him. They would shout he was *loco* (crazy, in a good way) and other insults; Luis did not care because he just wanted to be a good footballer; he wanted to play for Nacional because he was fanatical about the team. In the end he did it but not without great sacrifice.'

'El Principito' ('the Little Prince'), as he was known to the Uruguayan fans, paused for a moment, sipped a bit of

Coke and then smiled before adding: 'Most people would not have even bet $10 on that kid, and yet ...'

What did you teach him?
'I taught him what I like teaching all kids: how to turn on the spot with your shoulders to the goal, how to kick with decision and precision, how to head from a cross from a corner kick or a running cross, how to react as quickly as possible when a ball arrives at your feet when you are least expecting it. All kids in South America, including here [Uruguay] are born with a ball under their arm as a football is the first thing that a parent buys their son. Daughters get a Barbie. Times have changed but there is no greater present than a football. A PlayStation will not even get a look in. It is this first present which sets off the passion for the beautiful game. However, if you want to make it your living, you need to work hard.'

You played in Spain, Italy and Germany. How is it moving from Uruguay to Europe as a young 19-year-old?
'I also moved to Europe when I was very young. When I arrived at Zaragoza, I was eighteen ... But for us footballers, we do not make these calculations, we do not think about where we play, we just love football and this failsafe which you carry inside helps you wherever you are. I ended up in China at one point. What we Uruguayans have is this cheekiness, the football from the streets, from the makeshift pitches, but when we emigrate we have to become professionals because our football is excellent for technique and passion but tactically it is nowhere near as good as in Europe. When we go to Europe, we have to adapt. When I arrived at Real Zaragoza, for example, I started to train in a way that I had never trained before. I lifted weights, 120kg. I only weighed 70kg. I grew stronger and had greater stamina and the defenders

found it harder to push me over. Over a period of two years in Europe, I built up my physique and learnt the tactics. I remember Giuseppe Materazzi, the Lazio coach, who told me we play 4-4-2 and I did not even know what that meant. He told me that I had to run back and defend in midfield and I told him that I had come to Rome to score goals, not to defend. We have the physique, a canny ability and we adapt better than Brazilians to any championship because when we sign for a club, we honour the contract. This is why you find Uruguayan players all over the place. Those in the top leagues in Europe, sooner or later burst on to the scene at the highest level, just like Suárez. He wanted to show the world what he was made of, that his football could work anywhere. And he has done that.'

What type of player is he?
'He is the sort of player who fights for every ball for 90 minutes, he gets stuck in with the opponents, he falls and gets up, he throws himself into the penalty area. He is not a forward who waits for the ball to land at his feet, the perfect assist. No, Luis never stands still: he goes back and then pushes up front again. Does he have a refined technique? No, his ball control is normal but he knows how to push upfield, he knows how to progress and he has adapted his game.

'He has matured a great deal. When he gets shown the yellow card now, he controls his emotions whereas before he would blow his top and argue with the referee. Now before he overdoes it on the dribbling, trying to shimmy round a player and losing the ball, he will pass it to an unmarked teammate. He knows what he can give to the team. He is a great free-kick taker, his strike of the ball is excellent.

'Luis is a kid who has always wanted to improve; he has always trained hard and put in extra time. Not like lots of players who as soon as the training is over would make an excuse and head home. At Nacional, he would stay behind and take free-kicks or study how to get past the wall on a free-kick or practise volleys. You would have to kick him out most days. If you didn't, he would have stayed there. His football is not easy on the eye; he is not Messi. He is all about scoring goals; he plays a goalscorer's football and wherever he plays he scores a basketful of goals. To my mind, he who scores the most is the best. Suárez is a player who is capable of breaking boundaries and covering new ground. You have to give him credit for his consistency, his grit and determination and his will to get to the top of the top. It is a marvellous surprise for those, like us, who have trained him, helped him grow and develop as a player; it is worth repeating the fact that he has improved because he has a true passion for football, he lives for it – it is what makes him happy. Therefore, for what he has achieved with the national team in the World Cup in 2010 and the Copa América in 2011, he is an idol. In Uruguay, there are 3 million coaches, critics and sports commentators. Each has their own opinion, with their own formation, with their tactics, with their favourite forward, but Luis Suárez has made everyone agree for once.'

Chapter 6
A love story

They were both really young. She was twelve and he was fifteen. They saw each other for the first time at Fabric, a night club in Montevideo which puts on a matinée for kids. The matinée goes on from late afternoon until midnight. It was here that Luis met a beautiful blonde girl introduced to him by the boyfriend of one of her sisters. El Salta was not the prettiest of the bunch (his mates ribbed him constantly for his two front teeth and his cauliflower ears) but he was a nice guy, funny and knew how to charm the ladies. With his jokes and his confident manner, he won the heart of his little blonde sweetheart. The two of them started going out. Sofia Balbi, the girl in question, started turning up to Luis' training sessions and the Nacional youth matches. Those close to Luis knew that he was madly in love. You could see it a mile off. He never took his eyes off her. Wilson Píriz remembered a game he played with Suárez. I told him: 'If you score a goal you can have a few more pesos in your wage slip. It was like a red rag to a bull. Suárez gave his all to score a goal. He earned those extra pesos so he could invite Sofia to dinner and buy her a gift.'

Luis wanted to show her that he was mad about her and that he wanted to be with her. Sofia was a young girl but she was mature and down to earth. She was to become the help and support that Luis Suárez needed and had not had up to that point. This was something very important for Suárez, for his soul, and to keep his feet on the ground. She was not part of the footballing family; she was not part of that world; she was not one of his usual friends. Maybe it was for this reason that Luis listened to the little blonde girl with the ponytail and took her advice to heart. Sofia told him: 'Don't give up on school, keep going.' Luis took this on board and started studying. Sofia told him he could make it as a footballer and he started training even more than before and scoring more goals than before. Sofia comforted him, egged him on and did everything that was necessary to help him achieve his goal. Luis, for his part, gave his all; he put his heart and soul into the game and studied as hard as he could. The timing was crucial as Luis was going through a difficult time on the pitch and in the classroom. He believed in her; his little fairy whom he met on that magical summer's evening. She believed in him and she made him whole; she gave him that love that he yearned for.

Everything was going perfectly in this love story. The photos from that time show them arm in arm, smiling, cheek to cheek, two teenagers who had found happiness by being together. Everything was fine until the day when the bombshell was dropped: she was leaving for Europe. It was October 2004. Her family, who had been hit hard by the financial crisis in Uruguay which had crippled the middle class, decided to move to Barcelona in Spain. The day she left was the saddest day, for him and for her. The evening before her departure was even worse. Together, hand in hand, they walked the streets of Montevideo. They sat down at a bus stop and talked and talked without realising how much time had gone by. They cried. They thought they would never see each other again. Their goodbye was to be a long farewell. Luis was sixteen and he would not be able to afford the visits. Sofia was in the same boat. They thought that the distance would destroy their relationship and what they had been through and that they would go their separate ways. It was over.

Luis went all the way to Carrasco International Airport but he did not dare go in to say goodbye to Sofia. He cried his eyes out on the bus from the airport to his home. He was convinced that he had lost the love of his life and that he would never again see the woman who was key to his existence. He arrived at home with a large tiger cuddly toy he had bought for her. He threw himself on his bed and cried for hours. His heart was broken. He thought long and hard about calling it all off and going back to Montevideo, to his mum, his friends, Nacional and Sofia.

After a while, however, the daily routine eased the pain and the heartache. And his relationship with Sofia carried on – from a distance. The calls at night were long, there were lots of emails. The two had a lot to talk about. Sofia told him about her new life in Cataluña – her studies, her dreams, her family – and encouraged her love to carry on with his dreams and his passion, football. Luis was working hard, harder than he had ever worked before. He understood that football was his future, his life, maybe one day his career – and even a way to get his *belle* back. He knew they had to be together and that he wanted to wake up next to her every day. This is what he did.

Luis made his mark in the Nacional youth team and started earning some money. He spoke to his team managers with Daniel Fonseca, his agent, and found the money to go to Spain at the end of the year. This plane ticket for Barcelona became the focus of the year. Eduardo Ache, an economist, ex-senator of the Coloured Party, ex-minister of the Eastern Republic for the Coloured Party, Chairman of Nacional, remembers that eighteen-year-old as if it were yesterday: 'I ribbed him a lot, I made fun of him, I told him that he was a fatty, that he could not score in a month of Sundays … Suárez always had a comeback: "Chairman, today I will score but you have to pay for a plane ticket to Barcelona." Suárez scored and ran over to remind me of the bet. I had no choice but to buy him the ticket … Sofia even then was a pillar in his life'.

Luis and Sofia were apart for nearly two years. Then the Nacional number 9 received an offer from FC Groningen, a Dutch club. Holland was not Spain but Groningen was nearer to Barcelona.

Luis Suárez accepted and would later explain: 'If Sofia had been in Uruguay, I may not have made the decision I made'.

He flew to Europe and signed the contract with the Dutch club. The club gave him twelve days off. The first thing he did was get on a plane to Ciudad Condal. Moving to the Netherlands was not easy. He wanted to have Sofia by his side. This seemed complicated as Sofia was only 16. However, the Balbi family had adopted El Salteño right from the first moment. Sofia's father gave his blessing. He gave her permission to leave but he wanted to know when she would be back in Barcelona.

Sofia packed a few things in her suitcase, enough for a few days, and headed off. It was not long before Groningen was home for Sofia. The two were finally together after a lot of suffering. A dream which they had been nurturing for a long time had finally come true. Having her by his side meant everything to him. It meant he had a partner by his side who could help him give his all. As Luis has always said, if he is not happy off the pitch, he is not happy on the pitch.

The couple moved from Groningen to Amsterdam when Luis signed for Ajax. It was there, in March 2009, that he and Sofia got married. It was an intimate civil ceremony with a few friends and family and teammates. At the end of the season, the pair went on honeymoon to French Polynesia. On 26 December, the pair gave their vows in church and had a big reception in Montevideo.

Sofia wore a stunning traditional white dress, whereas Luis wore a black tuxedo and waistcoat with white shirt and tie. The newlyweds were splashed all over the front cover of Uruguay's *Caras* magazine. The exclusive photoshoot included a photo of a football. The subtitles under the photos confirmed that Sofia and Luis were expecting their first child. Delfina was born in Barcelona on 5 August 2010.

The day before the birth Luis was playing, and scored, during a Champions League qualifier against PAOK. Ajax chartered a private jet so Luis could get to Ciudad Condal for the birth. At 4.30 in the morning, Sofia gave birth to a beautiful baby girl. Luis commented: 'There is no greater emotion than seeing the entry into the world of your son or daughter. It is something I will never forget.'

Sixteen days later Delfina was presented to the Dutch fans in the Amsterdam arena. Delfina made the front cover of *Caras* at only two months old.

From Holland to England, from Amsterdam to Liverpool. On 26 November 2013, Benjamin, Luis and Sofia's second child, arrived. Luis gave the news by stuffing the ball up his Uruguay shirt during a match. Benjamin gets the special treatment at the tender age of ten days sporting a white bonnet with a Liverpool shirt. He is presented to the Liverpool fans before a match against Crystal Palace. Luis has two kids that he adores and that he brings to as many matches as he can. Selfies abound with Delfina and Benja.

And Sofia? The loved-up couple have been together for fourteen years now – fourteen fundamental years in Suárez's career.

How many times has Suárez said it, how many times has he repeated those words: if Suárez has been successful in football, it is all down to Sofia. Without her, without her by his side, her help, he may not have made it. Sofia knows him better than anyone else. She knows his weaknesses and his strengths and how to handle him. She gives him the stability he needs. Sofia has always watched him play and is his biggest critic. Sofia does not mince her words after a match, especially if he has not performed as well as she believes he should have. She is his biggest fan, be it from the sofa or the stands, she always puts her all into supporting Luis. She suffers like all the fans do when he loses. She is not the typical WAG who wants to be in the limelight or on the front of every gossip mag. She is a life companion, a partner, a support when the going gets tough for her man; she was at his side when he was insulted following the sendings-off and the biting incident. She was there for him when he had to stay away from the pitch. She told him several times: 'What do you think people think when they see you on the pitch, always on the edge; it looks as though you have the whole world against you. They don't know that at home you are a caring family man, calm and collected. You need to show this side of yourself to the fans.' How do you thank a lady who does all that for you? Love her to bits, cover the king-size bed with rose petals for your tenth anniversary, give her the attention she needs, kiss her after every goal, glance up at her every time you enter the pitch at Anfield and dedicate the PFA Player of the Year award for 2014 to 'my wife Sofia and my two little minions, Benji and Delfi, who I love very much'.

Chapter 7

Time bomb

'Of course I remember him! I saw him some times in the youth teams and then here, when he began playing in the first team. He was a little scrawny kid but he was already a solid player. Did they boo him? Not that I can remember. You would need to ask the Peñarol fans when Suárez scored a goal and we drew 2-2.'

During the break at Gran Parque Central, Héctor, an elderly fan, was drinking coffee and chatting with friends Augustín and Diego. Their team, Nacional, had not won for seven games and indeed had lost six on the trot. The 22,000 capacity stadium had areas where there were no spectators at all. Ten thousand were watching at most. Only the Banda del Parque end, where the *hinchas* (hardcore supporters) stand was, was full. The ultras had not stopped singing the whole first half. It was an autumnal day with the weather changing from one moment to the next: sun, then dark clouds, rain, rainbows spurting out from behind buildings on the skyline. The debate in the stands carried on. The topic? Suárez. Heads were getting hot and tempers bothered. The debate stopped when the players ran back on the pitch for the second half. Nacional was playing against Defensor Sporting. It was the last chance in the Closing Tournament, the last train to be able to fight for the championship. Carlos De Pena took the lead for the *Bolsos* in the 29th minute but the match was not over. There were still 45 agonising minutes to go.

It was against Defensor on 4 December 2005 when Luis Suárez won the hearts and minds of Nacional once and for all. The Nacional fans are demanding; they not only want to win but they want to see beautifully played football. The fans can leave the stadium at any moment if they do not like what they see on the pitch. They are passionate followers of football, unlike the Peñarol fans who are unforgiving of their players.

Suárez's debut in the first team was far from Montevideo in Barranquilla, the capital of the Colombian region of the Atlantic. On the evening of 29 April 2005, Luis played in the Luis Franzini Stadium for the second team against Defensor and he scored. The next day he entered the pitch during the second half against Danubio in the Della Valle Stadium and celebrated another goal with his teammates from the fourth team (Under-18s). At the end of the match, they told him he had to go to *Los Céspedes*, the Nacional training camp, which was a few miles outside Montevideo, at 3.00pm. He left with the first team for Barranquilla. Three days later, on 3 May, Nacional were playing against Junior in a Copa Libertadores second leg match. There was no way they could qualify for the last sixteen as they had only won one of the five matches played up to that point. The eighteen-year-old Suárez was allowed to play to gain experience and make up the numbers.

The heat in the Metropolitano Roberto Meléndez stadium was unbearable. The 16,000 spectators could not believe their eyes. The Uruguayans won with goals from Chori Castro, now at Real Sociedad, and Juan Albín, the latter in the 83rd minute. The score: 2-1. The *Tiburones* ('Sharks') risked not getting through the round. No one even noticed the kid who in the 75th minute came on for Sebastián Vázquez to head up the Uruguayan attack on the right. The Colombians were there holding their breath, hoping for a miracle. The Argentinian coach of Junior, 'El Zurdo' López, started to get worried and began to shout, bang his fists and wolf whistle. He gave orders left, right and centre from the bench. In the end, his players woke up. Hayder Palacio converted a penalty in the 85th minute: 2-2. In stoppage time, Martín Arzuaga scored for 3-2. Junior went through to the next stage of the Copa Libertadores. Nacional came in last and went home with their tail between their legs. Party time on one side and long faces on the other.

For Suárez it was his first taste of playing in the first team shirt of the club of his dreams. Fifteen minutes to breathe in the wonder of international club football; fifteen minutes of a fairly uneventful performance. But the impression he gave his teammates and his coach, Martín Lasarte, was a good one. Those fifteen minutes for Luis were unforgettable. After the match he explained: 'I was relaxed and I enjoyed playing with the first team. I was not afraid and I did not even realise who I was up against.'

On 6 July 2005, Nacional became the league champions in Uruguay. Defensor Sporting refused to play the two-legged playoff due to mistakes by the referee which, according to Sporting, had prejudiced the outcome of Nacional's match against Rocha FC. The club went into party mode but Luis was not at the forefront. He would have to wait another year for that.

Ronda, Spain: 11 August 2005, the Ciudad del Tajo Trophy was being played. On the pitch at the Municipal Stadium, Sevilla FC were playing Nacional de Montevideo. It was a dry affair in the first 45 minutes. Not even one shot on goal. Things hotted up in the second half. Luis Fabiano put Sevilla in front from a penalty. A few moments later and Nacional pulled level from another penalty. This time

Gabriel Pablo Alfaro had elbowed Suárez leaving him with a cut across his face. Gabriel Álvez converted the kick for 1-1. The match turned wild after that. Three goals in the dying minutes. Antonio López scored a second for the Spaniards and Luis scored his first goal for Club Nacional de Fútbol. It was a splendid bicycle kick on the edge of the area which beat Palop. It looked as though the Ciudad del Tajo Trophy would be decided on penalties. However, Aranda had other ideas. In stoppage time, he struck the winning goal: 3-2. Sevilla won the trophy.

Nacional ended their Spanish tour there and headed home. On 25 August the Opening Tournament started. Luis was on the bench and only played for a few minutes. On 10 September at the Gran Parque Central, Luis was brought on for Gabriel Álvez, the captain. Nacional were winning 4-0 against Paysandú, a club from central Uruguay which no longer exists. At the end of the match, Lasarte was in no doubt that Suárez should be involved. He was wearing the number 13 on his back, a number which brought him good luck. A few seconds after having come on, his first touch ended in a goal for Luis. The first competitive goal of his professional career. It was the 82nd minute and Suárez booted the ball up the right wing for Vásquez to run on to. Vásquez made it and skipped past a defender, darted across into the area and from the byline crossed the ball. Romero jumped and headed whilst leaning on a player from the other team but it was too weak. Suárez capitalised on this and jumped and bicycle-kicked the ball into the goalmouth in spectacular fashion.

Ignacio Bordad, the goalkeeper for Paysandú, raised his hand to parry it and one of the defenders tried to head the ball away but it deflected onto the crossbar. Vásquez smacked the ball into the goal but one of the defenders blocked it with his hands. Vásquez screamed for handball and a penalty but Suárez was already on the rebound like a hungry vulture and let rip a missile into the top right corner of the goal. This one had to go in. And it did. Goaaal! Suárez reeled off and raised his index finger to the sky and then to the bench. The number 13 kissed his emblem on his shirt before being swamped by his teammates. He had scored, he had made an impression – but to be the lead forward he would need to wait another month or so.

He got his chance on 22 October against River Plate.

Central midfielder Fabián Coelho was not fit according to the team doctor. Martín Lasarte walked into the *Los Céspedes* training camp offices with his assistant coach, Juan Carlos De Lima. They were contemplating who could possibly replace Coelho: should it be a central midfielder or another forward? They examined their various options and then they turned to each other and said: 'What are we going to do? Shall we put the kid on?' They decided to do it. They rejigged the formation so that there were three central midfielders and three forwards. Suárez was to play as number 9, the linchpin in the attack.

He played well but he did not score. This went on for five matches in a row. Suárez was perfect but he did not score. The centre forward ought to have been in the box, turning and shooting or heading but Luis would get the ball 40 metres out from the opponents' goalmouth, run past two or three defenders and then when he got to the goalmouth he would mess it up again and again. The crowd were not behind him. They started to jeer and tease him every time he touched the ball; they did not want him as the main centre forward. It was hard to work out seeing how young he was and that he was playing in his home town. He was a homegrown star who had come through the ranks with flying colours. It was hard to understand why the *Bolsos* were so impatient. And yet this was how things were to pan out. They were tough weeks for Suárez. The media started to lay into him and call him wooden leg. Luis asked the coach whether he was going to be kept on in the first team and whether he would keep his lead centre forward position – i.e. was he going to back him and stand up for him?

Martín Lasarte stoically supported his man and put up with the criticism and the boos and whistles from the stands as he was convinced that his player was destined for greatness and that he was a time bomb waiting to explode. Suárez thanked him for his support. It was a really difficult time for Suárez. Many would have faltered. Luckily the famous match on 4 December 2005 was around the corner.

Nacional were using a 4-4-2 formation: Bava was in goal, Jaume, Pallas, Victorino Mansilla, Vanzini, Vásquez, Mendez, Silva, Castro and Suárez. Luis was on the right and was running rings around the defence. The opposing team had to try and come up with a solution and improvise to stop the Suárez onslaught. They tried but there was nothing they could do: on the stroke of the 60th minute, Suárez scored an incredible goal. Alberto Silva released the ball to the edge of the area where Luis was waiting with his back to goal. He controlled the ball with his left foot, skinned a defender who was stuck to him like glue and pinged a screamer at mid-height which goalkeeper Juan Guillermo Castillo, 'El Cabeza' ('the Head'), could get nowhere near to. The match ended in a draw – 2-2 –but it was Suárez's coming of age and a great relief for Lasarte. The 'little kid' had more than convinced those that mattered that he was worthy.

This was the turning point. From that time on, no one dared challenge his authority and boo or jeer him. He scored in the last game of the Opening Tournament against Danubio. In the Closing Tournament which started on 19 February 2006, he scored seven goals including one against eternal rivals Peñarol.

The bomb had exploded. And that was not all because in the final of the 2005/06 Uruguayo against Rocha FC Luis scored in both the home and away legs. In the first match, 'Luisito', as he was called by the TV commentators, obliterated García, who was coming off his line, with a lightning sprint 30 metres upfield and then a missile across the face of goal into the top corner. It was the third goal in a match which ended 4-1.

On 25 June 2006 at the Parque Central it was chucking it down for the return leg. Luisito opened the scoring with a superb goal: he gained possession of the ball amid three defenders and stormed off to the touchline with the ball glued to his foot. He cut back and let rip a cross-cum-shot which seared into the corner. Garcia had no chance. GOOOAAAAL! The Parque erupted in unison GOOOAAAAL! The TV commentators went ballistic, imitating the celebratory jig, the rain dance and the dance of the championship. Nacional won the title for the second year running. The party was held in a deluge of torrential rain but Luis was on cloud nine all the same as he had won his first title at the tender age of nineteen and he was undoubtedly the star of the tournament.

'What a man! What a champion! Luisito the barbarian!' shouted the radio commentators. Over 28 matches, Suárez, the beginner, scored twelve goals – only one fewer than Chori Castro (who played 34 matches). A new star was born. He had just started to shine and he was already on his way. Augustin commented at the end of the match: 'Unfortunately Luis did not play that much here. Us fans did not get to enjoy watching him play. It would be good if he came to finish his career off here at Nacional, just like Álvaro Recoba. He is not in great shape but when he does play he always gives us something to smile about.' Augustin, Héctor and Diego were on their way home after the match. The conversation continued. They were happy. Maybe the rainbow which had burst out from behind the houses, and those drops of rain, had brought good luck. After 36 days, Nacional had woken up from its hibernation and had started winning again. A clean 2-0 win for a team which looked like it had found its way again. The crisis was not over but it looked like things were on the up. In the mixed area on the first floor at Parque Central, the usual press song and dance was going on. In the tiny room, TV cameras and journalists were waiting for Gerardo Pelusso, the coach; others, behind a bar, waited patiently and tried to jostle for space so as to get a glimpse of Sebastian Coates, who had come back to play for Nacional after eight months away, and two goalscorers: Carlos De Pena and Juan Cruz Mascia.

Microphones were laid on the floor; live TV feeds were ready. One player after another gave their view on the match, on this key victory and where the team was headed. But what did they think about Suárez? De Pena, 22 years of age, an attacking central midfielder, was in a hurry. He had to go and see his friends play a match. That said, he had a few minutes to tell people what he thought of the great man: 'Suárez grew up here like me and I believe that he has learnt a lot whilst playing for Nacional. This club is a melting pot for great players. I like the way he is always hungry for victory and goals, his enthusiasm when playing and his intensity of play. He always pushes for more and this is something he has learnt while playing Uruguayan football and with Nacional.'

Mascia, 20 years of age, is a centre forward by trade who came through from university football and started at

Nacional in 2013 in the Libertadores Cup. The club has nothing but praise for the young player. They believe he is the most promising player Uruguay has. What did he think about Suárez? 'Luis is an example to admire and follow. We would all like to play like him. He is the forward I admire the most. I envy the way he pressures defenders, how he moves on the pitch, how he manages to skim past tackles despite being marked by two or three players and how he finishes. I also am jealous of the way he kicks the ball from all positions, both from dead-ball situations and when he is on the move. He is incredible! I was lucky enough to be able to train with him in the *Complejo Celeste* (national squad training centre). I was in the Under-20s, Luis was on his own and came to play with us. I must be honest: he impressed me. He was a really normal humble guy who just fought for every ball, even in training. He had a great attitude. When I started here in the main team, I failed to score in the first four or five matches. I made mistakes, the ball went the wrong side of the post or was pushed back over the line; basically I just could not score. The crowd booed me. They started to compare me to Suárez in his early days. Someone said to me, "Don't worry, the same happened to Luis but look where he is now."'

Chapter 8

No limits

A conversation with Martín Lasarte

He started life as a defender and now he is a coach. As a player with Nacional de Montevideo, he won the Libertadores Cup, the Intercontinental Cup, the Interamerica Cup and the South American Cup. He played in Spain; he was captain of Deportivo de La Coruña. La Coruña fans used to shout: 'Take the machete, Lasarte, take the machete'.

'Machete' is a nickname which people still remember today.

Martín Lasarte Arróspide, 54 years of age, born in Montevideo to a Basque father, smiled when he heard this. He has heard lots of things over his career when he marked the players of Deportivo, Nacional, Defensor Sporting, Rampla Junior and Rentista. He has heard even worse as a coach. His coaching career started in 1996 and saw him travel all over the world: from Uruguay to the United Arab Emirates, from Millonarios in Bogotá to Danubio, from Real Sociedad in San Sebastián to the Catholic University of Santiago in Chile. On 16 May 2014, after five months away from the bench, he signed a new contract to train Chile University. We met in a hotel bar in Montevideo to reminisce about the 2005/06 season when he won the Closing Tournament and played Luis Suárez.

Lasarte started setting out his view: 'Nacional is a club

which has always backed its pool of players. It is part of a sporting heritage and has a culture of sporting excellence which when I arrived I wanted to find out about and see what the youth teams were doing. I went to see a few matches with the youth teams and I asked Ricardo Perdomo what he thought about a few players. Regarding Luis, he was crystal clear: 'If you take him with you in the first team, you will not regret it. He will not let you down'. He was convinced and his conviction left its mark on me. It was a weekend and Suárez was in Spain, in Barcelona. He had gone to see Sofía. I remember that on the Monday we had back-to-back training sessions. That morning, Luis did not turn up. He got in on an Iberia flight at 1.30pm. But in the afternoon he came to training with the squad at *Los Céspedes*. From that moment on, he trained with us even if they asked him to play youth team matches.'

What type of eighteen-year-old was he?
'Shy but with a great personality. He seemed much more mature than his age. I believe he was forced to grow up before his time considering what was going on in his personal life. The fact that he was from central Uruguay, that he had to fight for his family, that he had to bring home the money, that he had to make his way in a big city like Montevideo and that he had to make it at football. One thing is certain: he believed in himself, he was sure of his abilities. He led a normal life with his mother and brothers. At the time, he already had an agent, Daniel Fonseca, who looked after him and made sure he had boots and shirts and other clothing, and who took him to Holland. Physically he was strong and stocky and could put on the pounds if he was not careful. In fact I was surprised when he came back from Groningen, he was so thin and sinewy.'

And what about his technical ability?

'He had those features that a special player has, he was impressive. Those key skills are still the same. He has just improved them and fine-tuned them. He has worked on them bit by bit. He is good at shaking off an opponent. He has great dribbling skills. Luis is better in the open spaces rather than close-quarter combat. He has a great shot on the run and from dead-ball situations. I remember one of the goalies at training at *Los Céspedes* used to say to me that Suárez should take the kicks as the others were clueless compared to him. He has a great game in the air even if he does not score that often with his head. He is a forward who can move around the front line as he picks and chooses. He is capable of starting on the right and finishing on the left. Or vice versa. He is ambidextrous and finishes well with both feet. In Uruguay, he is thought of as a typical centre forward in the box, which is a simplification because he can play behind the number 9 as he does for the national team with Cavani, with whom he has a great feeling, and Luis can also come from deep, as he has shown many a time.'

Weak points?

'He used to fake injury or fouls; lots of referees used to fall for it and blew for the free kick, penalty or yellow card as dictated by the circumstances. He thought it would help the team but in the end the referees grew wise to his antics and they would punish him for it. He knew how to work the defenders on the opposing team; he had just the right amount of mischievousness to provoke them and to make them fall into his trap and then with an 'Olé' he would whizz round them leaving them standing. These are a forward's bread and butter, his tools of the trade which Luis was a master of from a very young age. Luis carries the weight of the history of Uruguayan football on his back and sometimes it can get a little too heavy but sometimes it gives him the positive impulse he needs. He was a good teammate and in the changing rooms there were never any issues, be it with white or coloured players.'

Did he ever have any issues with you?
'There was once when I reprimanded him during that season with Nacional. I cannot recall whether it was for his weight or for training where he did not give his all. I saw that he did not like it. He did not like being criticised and it hurt him to accept what I had said. I had been harsh on him but for a reason. I told him that if he carried on like that he would not be on the pitch on Sunday; it just slipped out. We had an argument but it was nothing. In the end Luis processed the information and understood where I was coming from and he reacted positively. That was the only argument I had with El Salta.'

What is the quality that you appreciate the most in Suárez?
'It is the fact that he knows no limits. He reacts even in the most difficult situations football can put you in. We would be losing and he would believe we could turn things around and win; he would be goalless but would say he knew he could score. He never gave up or lowered his head. He feared nothing and no one. Would you like an example?

Sure.
'In the summer of 2005, we went to La Coruña in Spain where I had played for four years. We were playing the Teresa Herrera Trophy. It was a three-team affair:
     Deportivo, Peñarol and Nacional. Against Deportivo, Luis was up against a defender whose name I forget. He was

a big guy, strong and experienced who had been around the block. Suárez tricked him two, three, four, five times and was not intimidated. Three months later, Lendoiro, the chairman of Deportivo, called me looking for a forward. He asked about Luis. I told Augusto that he was still a bit young to be heading off to Europe but he was ready technically. The chairman was impressed by that kid who was not afraid to take on a defender who was much older and more experienced.'

What about the jeers and boos against Luis in Gran Parque Central. How do you remember that moment?
'I always remember the face of a Nacional fan ... what I heard them saying should not be repeated. I never understood why they had it in for him. It all started with the match against River. Luis created ten or twelve chances but messed up the final pass, the shot, you know, he failed to put the ball in the back of the net. The insults started but Luis managed to quieten the critics. His goals and moves saw to that. At the end of the season he was an idol for the fans.'

Did the fact that Luis left at the end of the season surprise you?
'This is the reality of Uruguayan football. As soon as a good player comes of age, there is someone ready to take them away from you. It was a question of finances at the end of the day; I am not sure if Nacional had to pay off some debts or whether it was an agreement with his agent. The fact is that I had him in my team for six to eight months as a project and three to four as a fully fledged player.

'I recall saying to Ricardo Alarcón, the future chairman of Nacional, that it would be good to build a team around Suárez, similar to what Peñarol had done with Morena. We had up and coming juniors like Chori Castro, Albín,

Victorino, Diego Godín and Sebastián Viera; the potential was there. With a few experienced players we could have built something special. But it was not possible; in Uruguay it is difficult to plan for the future of a club. In fact, the next time round they sold Godín, Albín and Chori Castro.'

Have you kept in touch with Luis after he went?
'I was playing at *padel* (a game like squash) Punta del Este and the phone rang. It was Luis. In *Marca* [a Madrid sports daily] news had come out that I had been offered the chance to go and manage Deportivo La Coruña. Suárez was dead keen to go to Spain. I told him that unfortunately it was just a rumour and that no one had called me. I told him I would take him with me, of course. Then he left for Ajax and I went to Real Sociedad.

I met him on the plane to Europe. He had to change in Madrid. Pere Guardiola, his agent, brother of Pep, was there. We talked about lots of things, seeing as several Spanish media had asked who I preferred for Barcelona between Alexis Sanchez and Luis Suárez. I had no doubts. During the flight, we got chatting about Barcelona and the Spanish league. He was interested in trying to secure a place at Barça. However, circumstances dictated that he ended up at Liverpool. And look, now he is a Barcelona player. And last season demonstrated that he is able to improve with other stars around him. In Uruguay, we have had great footballers who have made it abroad like Enzo Francescoli, Rubén Sosa, Álvaro Recoba, Paulo Montero, Daniel Fonseca, El Pato Aguilera, but none of them have made it to the top of the world rankings. Luis could do it. There are no limits.'

Chapter 9

In the city of the north

Stalls of fish, fruit, veg; stalls of coloured tulips, clothes, shoes; stalls of various cheeses of all shapes and sizes; stalls of chairs and wooden stools all awash with the smell of fried prawns coming from the huge bubbling pans. It was market day in Grote Markt in Groningen. People were hunting for bargains, buying things or just browsing. There were those who were eating *bacalao* under white marquees. In Vismarkt Square, there were those who were waiting in front of a Belgian food van for a bag of chips drowned in ketchup and mayonnaise. Some were tempted by the meat *empanadas* from the Venezuelan food van. The Martinitoren, the bell tower of St Martin's church, which rises 100 metres into the sky and is over 500 years old, cast its shadow over the square and over the ancient post office building (now transformed into a supermarket) crowned by Hermes, the Greek god. Grote Markt was and is the beating heart of the city.

On foot from the central station, it took ten minutes. A quick trip across the canal on a bridge and Groninger Museum was right there. There were two pavilions, one opposite the other, designed by Alessandro Mendini and Philip Stark. The red writing on the grey cylinder of the museum: '*De student in Groningen 1614–2014*' ('student in Groningen 1614–2014') revealed the identity of this little Amsterdam-esque city in the north of the Netherlands. It has been a university town for 400 years or so. Theology and medicine are the subjects most famously studied here. Fifty thousand students inhabit the place, out of a total population of 198,000. Groningen is the youngest city in Holland with an average age of 35. The youngest and the most cyclable in the world: 57 per cent of trips made in the city are by bike. One does not need to view the statistics to realise this. A quick look around and there is not a street without bikes or bike parks on it. A trip along De Herestaat says it all. Low, coloured houses, shops, nineteenth-century coffee houses, no cars and bikes everywhere. An historic centre surrounded by canals. Beyond the canals to the east, the new residential areas, skyscrapers, green parks and the Euroborg, the stadium of FC Groningen, the Eredivisie (Dutch first division) team. The stadium is a white and green cathedral which is home to a school, a multiplex cinema, offices, a casino, a Chinese restaurant, a gym, a supermarket and stands for 22,000 spectators. Opened by Arjen Robben on 13 January 2006 before the match against SC Heerenveen.

Six months after the opening, Luis Suárez joined FC Groningen. The club was founded in 1971 and has not won national or international trophies; it floats around the middle of the table of the Eredivisie. Its glory moment was the Koeman saga: Martín the father, Ronald and Erwin the sons. The club has not played much in Europe but the 2006/07 season saw them qualify for the UEFA Cup after a fourteen-year wait.

The story of how 'El Salta' made it to Europe and turned up in a city in the north of the Netherlands, a quiet and tranquil city, is a long story, encompassing scouting, financial problems, football agents, love, and long deals to secure exorbitant fees. It is a story which can be told from a Dutch and a Uruguayan perspective.

Eduardo Ache, chairman of Nacional, sipping an

Amaretto di Saronno with orange juice in the Hotel Carrasco bar, gave his version of events: 'The first offer for Suárez was from Flamengo: a million dollars for 50 per cent of the player's rights. We passed the offer to Luis who rejected it as he did not want to go to Brazil. Luis asked us to speak to his agent, Daniel Fonseca, who refused the deal which would have favoured Nacional. There was also interest from Anderlecht in Belgium but Luis was having none of it for the same reasons that the player refused other offers: his agent did not like the offer. After a while, the offer from Groningen came through. We could do nothing as the deal was in the hands of those who were not with our club. The deal was closed by Ricardo Alarcón who replaced me as chairman of Nacional. Both he and I were distraught as we did not want to sell a player that young with that much potential. Luis had a great future ahead of him but the finances of the club had borne the brunt of the 2001 and 2002 crisis. We were not in good shape financially. In those situations you are pushed around by the agents and representatives of the player who own the rights to the player.' This was the Uruguayan version of events. What was the Dutch version?

FC Groningen were looking at markets where they could get good players at competitive prices. If PSV was renowned for looking at Brazil (just think of the likes of Ronaldo Luís Nazário de Lima or Romario), if Ajax looked to Denmark and AZ Alkmaar to Belgium, Groningen was one of the first Dutch teams to scout out the Uruguayan market. In 2005, they took Bruno Silva from Danubio. Silva was a right-back. Groningen had also taken Pablo Lima, a left-back, from Danubio of Montevideo. Although the Lima deal did not turn out as planned, a year later, Grads Fühler, a talent scout, and Hans Nijland, sports manager for Groningen, went back to the Eastern Republic in Uruguay. The goal was to find a number 9 who was tall, strong and powerful: specifically, they were looking at Elias Ricardo Figueroa. Elias was seventeen years old but he had already started for 'Liverpool' of Montevideo in the Opening Tournament. In 2005, in the South American category, he scored six goals making him one of the most promising Uruguayan players. The two representatives from Groningen went to watch him play at Liverpool. The impression the player made was not great; he seemed too immature, indecisive, not aggressive enough, but for the moment he was still a possibility. Everything changed when one Saturday the two reps went to see Nacional against Defensor. It was there that they saw someone who did impress them with the way he played. He played like a man possessed: he fought for every ball, caused chaos in the opponents' defence and to top it all off he put one in the back of the net. It was Luis Suárez of course.

Fühler and Nijland were convinced they had found what they were looking for: a rough diamond. They did not want to let him sign for another club. Gustavo Nikitiuk, Figueroa's agent (who had convinced the Dutch to see his man play), gave Groningen's men the contact details of Daniel Fonseca. This was the start of a long, drawn out and at times ridiculously complicated negotiation between the agent and the club. The numbers being bandied about were around the million to a million and a half dollar mark. This was an amount which was beyond the reach of the Dutch club. It was only thanks to a group of private investors that Groningen could get the ball rolling. The discussions with Daniel Fonseca and the Nacional management team were getting increasingly intense. The rub was the percentage that the tricolour club would get if Suárez was transferred to another club. The atmosphere was so tense that, on 2 July at the end of a qualifying match for the South American

Cup against Central Español, Lucho confessed to *El País* in Montevideo: 'I am very nervous and uptight because I want to leave. I want to transfer to Holland. It all depends on the response from Nacional. I trust that they will make the right decision for me and my family.'

The decision favoured the young Luis. On 4 July, Fonseca and Nacional smoothed out the last few differences and four days later the boy from Salto moved to Groningen. The deal was done. It was a transfer that left a bitter taste in the mouths of many fans and club officials. Nacional had got itself into a position where it was forced to sell its best players to buy other players and pay wages and bonuses. The coffers were empty and the membership subscriptions were not enough to keep the club afloat. Some commentators even spoke of the weakness of Uruguayan football and asked: 'Independiente sold Sergio Agüero for €23 million. Is there really €22 million difference between Suárez and Agüero?'

Luis Suárez was already in Europe. On 11 July 2006 he was presented to the club as the new FC Groningen signing. A photo taken after the signing of the contract, as he shook hands with Hans Njiland, shows Luis in a black suit, white shirt, brylcreemed hair with little waves in it and a toothy smile. When Groningen manager Henk Veldmate asked him, 'How many goals do you think you will score?', El Salta came straight back with 'Fifteen'. And when Veldmate, who was taken aback by the confident response of Luis, commented, 'Good, very good', Luis added, 'Yes but fifteen over the five years'.

Luis told the local media that Bruno Silva had spoken to him and told him what a great club it was, a great organisation with a magnificent stadium. Ron Jans, the Groningen coach, was satisfied with his new addition to the team. He was happy to have a key player like Luis in a tricky season in which the team was battling on three fronts: the league, the Dutch cup and the UEFA Cup. Luis would complement the existing attack of Erik Nevland and Glen Salmon. Everything seemed like it was going the way it was meant to for the nineteen-year-old Luis. He was on his way.

Hugo Alves Velame, Brazilian ex-central midfielder for Flamenco, Fluminense and Groningen (1997–2005), who is now coach of the Under-15 squad for the club, said: 'When Luis arrived at the club, he did not speak a work of Dutch or English and yet he would get what he wanted at the local supermarket by pointing and gesticulating or making up words until the person he was communicating with understood. This was incredible to me as I was a fish out of water in my first few days in Holland.' Alves spoke Portuñol and for this reason he was put in charge of helping Luis settle in. Luis would go twice a week to the 'Il Lago' restaurant to eat tortellini with cream, as Pino Camera, the owner, recalled. Alves explained what impressed him the most about the new arrival: 'He was spontaneous, sincere and talked to everyone in the same way, from the Queen of England to a tramp on the street. Everything is very organised here. Sometimes it is too organised for the South Americans; it is too quiet and relaxed. The players in the changing rooms are very discreet. Suárez was the complete opposite. He would turn up to training and be chatty, joking and singing; he would switch on the radio full blast just like a Brazilian. In less than a week, he knew the city better than me. He had asked that the club give him an automatic car. I am not sure if he had a driving licence. The fact is he did not know how to drive and every time he came back from a trip round the city, it had a few more dents than before he took it out. Whilst parking, he had bumped it against the other cars. He said: 'No worries, nothing serious. What does it matter?'

Bruno Silva, his compatriot, helped him to learn how to drive. He was more than a big brother to Luis (he is seven years older); he helped him settle in. Silva explained this in a hotel in Montevideo: 'I tried to make it easy for him, to explain the problems I had faced when I started for the club: the culture, the way of thinking, the training, the time-table, the discipline, the food, all things which when taken together became a big mountain to scale.' The beginning was not easy for Luis at Groningen. He was overweight. The nutritionist for the club put him on a diet. Sofia, his fian-cée, was asked to make sure he did not eat any more pizza, Coke – just water, water and more water. So much so that Suárez would recall some time later: 'Water poured out of my pores'. Every Friday Luis was weighed on the scales and if he had not lost the weight, he would not play. The hard training sessions took their toll on his body. Silva gave an example: 'You had just two touches of the ball, run round the cones that the trainer had set out on the pitch. You needed to do exactly as you were told. Luis did it right the first time; the second time, he only touched the ball once as he would have done when he was back in Uruguay. The trainer saw him and made it clear he was not happy with Luis's attitude. Another example? The coach gave him some advice on a particular point on his position on the field, Luis acknowl-edged as though he had understood but still did his own thing on the pitch.' He trained with the first team but played with the reserves. His teammates didn't quite get him. They thought that the guy who walked around with a thermos in his hand with his *mate* (caffeine-infused drink) in it was a bit odd. They had not even heard of him, they did not know him and they certainly did not view him as a talent. Sander Rozema, one of his teammates in the reserve team, now cen-tre midfield for Emmen, came back from training and said to his dad, confused: 'They spent a load of cash for a South American who is pretty second rate. He does not even know how to kick the ball.' The masseurs said the same thing to Hugo Alves but he quipped: 'Just wait and you will see that he is the best player that Groningen has had.'

Not many believed him. They were used to a striker with a different style from that of Suárez. Not a player who argued with the referee, faked fouls and who on the pitch never stopped goading, complaining, talking and shouting. Many snubbed him and underestimated him. Luis was disappointed. This was not what he was expecting. He dreamed of Europe, noisy bustling stadiums and cheering fans; instead he had to settle for a provincial stadium with not many spectators. He had few stints in the first team. Three minutes as a substitute for Salmon against Feyernoord in the first Eredivisie game on 20 August 2006. It was his first match for the first team. Not much happened.

On 14 September 2006, he finally got his chance. Wearing the green shirt with number 20, El Salta played his first match in Europe. It was in Belgrade against Partizan in the first round of the UEFA Cup. Luis came on in the 73rd minute for Koen van de Laak. The score was heavily in favour of the home team: 4-1. More importantly Luis scored in stoppage time. The ball, which was flicked on by Erik Nevland, landed with Luis who was with his back against a defender; he crafted a lob which went over the head of the goalkeeper, who had anticipated a low shot. Bruno Silva went to celebrate the goal but the match was over. In the return match, Groningen won 1-0 but were out of the European tournament.

Luis was not happy. He felt misunderstood. He was fighting for a place in the first team but he was not being given the chance to make his mark. A few minutes here and there and then he was back with the reserves. Hugo Alves reported that Ron Jans, the coach, would lose his rag with Luis. He would bring him off the pitch and put him on the bench because he was not playing how he wanted Luis to play and because he was arguing with all and sundry. When Luis started to gesticulate at the bench, that was it. Luis was off and he left the pitch without even shaking hands with his teammates and headed for the showers. It was raining and the coach was so angry that he threw an umbrella at him. The next Sunday he lent him the umbrella and made him do a lap of honour of the pitch in front of thousands of enthusiastic fans. It was to be a miracle of a match, as Luis and Sofia would later call it.

Bruno Silva recalled: 'The coach called me during the week. He wanted me to explain to him that in Holland you cannot behave the way he was behaving; you cannot fake fouls, dive and feign injury to get a free kick or a penalty. You cannot argue with the referee all the time. He told me that he respected his style, his aggression on the pitch but that is not how football is played in Holland and that was that. Luis shook his head. He thought for a minute and then retorted: "Tell him to put me in the first team, put me in the lead centre forward position." Jans laughed out loud. Luis kept on telling him the same thing. Luis told me to tell him that if he did not play a good match then he could send him back to Uruguay. The coach listened to him and Luis played as though his life depended on it.' It was 1 October 2006. Groningen was playing at home against Vitesse. It was Groningen's sixth league match of the season. Suárez, wearing number 9, led the attack against the black and yellows. The match started and things were not looking good for the boys in green. Anduele Pryon, the number 30 for Vitesse, was completely unmarked in front of the goal and connected with a cross from the right to head home. In the 31st minute, Suárez was tripped in the penalty area. The referee did not blow his whistle for a penalty. To top it all off, Suárez was booed by the rival fans. What a drama queen! Two minutes later El Salta was involved in the midst of the action again. He sprinted up the wing on the left, skimmed past a defender, cut into the area and screamed a missile towards the top right corner, which the Vitesse goalkeeper just managed to tip over the bar. In the 39th minute came the equaliser, from Levchenko. It did not last long: Youssuf Hersi scored a double to take a 3-1 lead for Vitesse. This was not good and Jans was extremely agitated on the touchline. There were only ten minutes left. Suárez moved up a gear. In the 80th minute, he was pulled down in the area and this time Suárez got the penalty. Koen van de Laak converted for 3-2. In the 89th minute, Luis ended up with the ball at his feet somehow and scored the equaliser for 3-3. He celebrated by blowing kisses to the crowd from the edge of the pitch. The match was not done yet. In the 91st minute, Suárez controlled the ball in the middle of the pitch, hustled past a midfielder and with his left foot pinged the ball into the back of the net. The Euroborg stadium went wild and erupted in cries of joy; Luis' teammates tackled him to the ground and smothered him in a group hug which went on for several minutes. Groningen were only one point away from Ajax at the top of the table. This was Suárez's moment. He had finally proved his worth in Europe. It had taken some time but it had finally arrived. He had had to decipher the code of the players, work out what made them tick and behave in a certain way. Erik Nevland commented on the event as follows: 'After that match, he started to play stunning football. It was incredible what he did on the pitch.'

Bruno Silva added: 'Luis is one of those players that I

saw grow up so quickly. It is all his doing. We should not forget that. When he arrived at Groningen, he told me that he did not know how to shoot from a long way back, that he always scuffed it. After training, he would stay behind on his own and keep practising shots from a distance. He scored two goals like that for Groningen that season.' Within a few months he was a hero for the Groningen fans and a villain for the other teams in the league. He was given seven yellow cards and one red. He made an impression for his style of play, his determination.

Life was looking up for Luis both on and off the pitch. Off it, he moved from his city centre apartment to a residential area in the south of Groningen near the lake where other players lived in new builds. Sofia moved from Barcelona to live with him. They got on famously. She helped with daily life, cooking and dealing with chores. Luis swore he would help out as soon as he could. He missed his family and Rio de La Plata but his mother and brothers did see him every now and then. He studied Dutch with a teacher provided by the club. Bruno Silva recalled his life as 'a low-key life, perhaps a bit monotonous, with training, *mate*, matches, family meals and *asados* (BBQs) improvised on electric grills which filled the house with smoke'.

At the end of the season, Groningen were eighth in the table. Suárez had scored ten goals in 29 matches (three fewer than the top goalscorer Nevland). He had transformed from street player to football player. An all-round footballer. A *Rummelaaetje* (a hustler) as the Dutch call it. Ajax had him in their sights.

Chapter 10

Red and white

9 August 2007: AFC Ajax and FC Groningen announced that they had reached an agreement for the 'immediate transfer' of Luis Suárez to Ajax. The contract is a five-year contract. This was the final element of a story which had kept pundits guessing, writing columns and giving interviews for weeks. What was going on? Simple: the performances of a young kid from Uruguay in a provincial team had attracted the interest of the mighty and powerful in the Eredivisie. Ajax had sold Ryan Babel to Liverpool for £11.5m and were looking to get their hands on the number 9 from Groningen. Luis was a perfect replacement for Babel who had left for the green pastures of England. The initial offer of €3.5m was rejected. The management of Groningen were not of the opinion that this amount reflected the market value of a player who had achieved what he had achieved for the club. It was not just a question of money either. *El Salta* had won over the fans and the coach. Groningen were not that keen on selling him. Despite Luis having sworn he was loyal to Groningen, he was intrigued by the opportunity to play for the Amsterdammers. When the TV interviewed him, he simply stated: 'Who wouldn't want to play for Ajax?'

It was a stalemate. The player wanted to go but the club wanted to keep him. Bruno Silva advised Luis to keep calm. He told Luis it was for the club management and the agents to sort out. But Luis was worried; he wanted to know what was going on and where his future lay. It was a future that was to be decided in the KNVB (Dutch Football Association) offices. Suárez and his agent tried to force Groningen's hand. Via his lawyers, they took the case to a federal arbitration. They argued that a move to Ajax would lead to an improvement in Suárez' economic and sporting conditions. Would the federation see it the same way?

The decision of the 'committee of the wise men' was not in Luis' favour. The reasons given by the player for the transfer to Ajax were picked apart as follows: Groningen was in the same league as Ajax and so there would be no improvement in Luis' sporting conditions, and there would be no improvement in his economic position as Groningen had offered him a new contract for more or less the same figure as that of Ajax.

One thing was clear: the whole palaver had damaged the relationship the player had with Groningen's management and the fans of the club. Thus it was, when Ajax proposed a new offer for €7.5m, the green and white club considered it was a fair offer and accepted despite having won the arbitration. They had got their capital back with decent interest! It was better to cash in and move on to avoid problems in the future with a player who did not want to stay at the club. The two sports directors, Maarten Fontein and Hans Nijland, as a sign of goodwill stated that, due to the historic friendly relations between the two clubs, a positive outcome was achieved.

Everyone was happy, apparently. Suárez was the happiest of all. He got through the routine medicals and moved to his new team.

Luis stated that it was his dream to have made the transfer happen and that this was a great moment in his footballing career. Luis was happy to be able to play for one of the great European clubs.

Indeed, one of the greats. Ajax is the most successful club in Holland: 28 league titles, seventeen Holland Cups, four Champions Leagues and two Intercontinental Cups. It is the team which revolutionised the world of football with the 'total' football of Rinus Michels and which left fans spellbound in the 1960s and 1970s; it is the club where the likes of Johan Cruyff, Ruud Krol, Marco van Basten, Frank Rijkaard, Edwin van der Sar, Clarence Seedorf, Edgar Davids, Zlatan Ibrahimović and Dennis Bergkamp have made their mark. And this is to name but a few. This list of champions which Ajax has been home to in its 114-year history is nothing short of incredible. In short, Ajax is a footballing force to be reckoned with, and critics feared that it was to be too big a force for a twenty-year-old who had only played one season in Europe. The critics expected *El Salta* to start on the bench and to get used to it. However, things were to turn out differently.

Luis could not play the Holland Supercup match against PSV on 11 July, which Ajax would win with a goal from Gabri. But on 15 August he was on the pitch. He would make his first appearance in a Champions League match against SK Slavia Praga in the Amsterdam Arena. He came on in the 72nd minute with number 16 on his back, replacing the Spaniard, Ismael Urzaiz. The match did not go well but Luis made a good impression.

Four days later, 19 August, he started for the first time. Ajax was playing the newly promoted De Graafschap. It was an annihilation: 8-1 to Ajax. *El Salta* certainly joined in the fun. He made the assist for the first goal and scored the second, his first with the red and white shirt on.

In the second league match in the Eredivisie against

SC Heerenveen he scored a double. On 29 August in the return leg of the Champions League in Prague against Slavia, he scored again. It was a shame that it was not enough to qualify for the next stage of the competition, as Ajax lost 2-1 to the Czech team. There was no doubting Luis had started on the right foot.

Henk ten Cate, the Ajax coach in 2007, the number two to Frank Rijkaard at Barcelona, summed it up as follows:

'We paid dearly for Luis, €7.5m, which is a high price for the Dutch market, especially for a young player who has still to show his worth. There was a risk, as had happened with lots of other kids of his age at the club, that he would not flourish, that he would not continue what he had started at Groningen. But this did not happen with Luis, he was excellent right from the very first match.'

Ten Cate recalled the first impressions which Luis made on him when he arrived at the club: 'He had a strong personality, he was an open book and very frank. What you see is what you get. Luis did not hold anything back. He was and is a winner, you could see it in his face. He was a kid from the streets who had learnt how to fight to survive and he showed it on the pitch, giving his heart and soul for every ball on the pitch. Obviously he had to adapt to the club, to its discipline and to the pressure which was loaded on to his shoulders. If you win at Groningen, great, if you lose, it is not the end of the world. For Ajax, you have to win every match, every competition and the league. If you don't, it is a failure.

'Suárez took his time to adapt to Ajax's style of play which was different to that of Groningen, where he was free to do what he wanted up front. Ajax has always played 4-3-3: four defenders, three midfielders and three forwards. Luis had to stick to his position and his role, even though it was not his way to stick to a fixed role and position. The fact that he was playing with great footballers and against quality opponents made him into what he is today, one of the best forwards in the world. We had Klaas-Jan Huntelaar in the number 9 position who had scored 36 goals in the previous season. To be honest, I have to say that the combo of Luis and Klaas-Jan up front was not the best ever. They were both young and got in each other's way a bit and each blamed the other for the missed goal or pass. Huntelaar was the star and, as with many young players, he was not happy that another player came to steal his limelight. Huntelaar and Suárez were two roosters in the chicken pen fighting for the number 1 spot. It was difficult to get these two to work together. In fact the best period for Suárez at Ajax started in December 2008 when Huntelaar left for Real Madrid.

'It was interesting watching them in the changing rooms and on the pitch. When Luis showed up he made it clear from the off what his role in the team was. He knew what he wanted.'

Ten Cate worked with Suárez for only four months. On 8 October 2007, Ajax announced he was leaving the team. He was headed for Chelsea as assistant manager to Abraham Grant, the coach who had inherited Mourinho's Chelsea. Before leaving he gave some parting advice to Suárez: 'I told him to be himself, to believe in his dreams and to not change his attitude on the pitch. For someone like Luis, all a coach can do is try and teach him tactics. You cannot tell him how to play the ball, he learnt that on the streets of Salto and Montevideo.'

Henk ten Cate's replacement was a homegrown choice: Adrie Koster, the man in charge of the Ajax youth teams. He was a good man who Suárez got on with. Step by step, match by match, Suárez started to fit in with Ajax's style of play and their formation, which rewards those players that play for the team and focuses on ball possession. He also tried to improve on his weaknesses.

He had worked very hard at Groningen with Raymond Libregts, the assistant coach there, to get rid of his tendency to dive and fake fouls.

Ronald de Boer, ex-midfielder for Ajax and Barcelona, brother of Frank de Boer, now coach for Ajax, commented on Luis' style as follows: 'It is part of his personality and his South American way of playing. Neymar was called a *cai cai* [diver], as was Cristiano Ronaldo when he moved to the Premier League. It is something which is in the DNA of a certain way of interpreting the game, in what the crowds from different countries want to see and in referees who are a bit more lax. It is hard to get rid of.'

The same applied when trying to keep Suárez quiet when a referee's decision did not go his way. In any event, at the end of Suárez' first season with Ajax, despite the fierce competition with his partner up front, he showed that he was a goal scorer: seventeen goals in the league (22 in total) against the 33 of Huntelaar (36 in total). Unfortunately the results of the team were not the best and Ajax ended the season in second place in the league table, just three points behind PSV. In the Cup, they went out in the last sixteen against NAC Breda. The worst memories from the season were the fall out with his teammate and the match against Groningen at the Euroborg stadium. Albert Luque, previously with Majorca and Deportivo La Coruña, moved to Ajax from Newcastle in August. He was a forward with a chip on his shoulder. He gave as good as he got. It was fisticuffs with Suárez all the time.

It was 11 November 2007 when the pair of them raised fists at each other. The team in red and white was playing Feyenoord at De Kuip, a difficult and tense match. In the 42nd minute, Luque caught Suárez, as was shown by the replay. The crop was a reaction to the 'rude gesture' of Suárez who did not give the ball back after a free-kick had been blown. At the end of the first half, the two players walked off the pitch yelling abuse at each other. In the changing rooms, things degenerated and fists were raised. The players' teammates intervened to calm things down. Adrie Koster, the coach, decided that to keep the peace neither player would be allowed back on the pitch for the second half. The next day, Martin van Geel, sports director, spoke to Suárez, who was in Uruguay for a World Cup qualifier, and to Luque and, after both players had apologised, he fined them for 'having brought the name of Ajax into disrepute and for having negatively impacted an important game for the club'. A wage cut but nothing more, and in the end things worked out. When Suárez goes to Barcelona to see Sofia's family, sometimes he meets up with his ex-rival.

What happened on 13 April 2008, the penultimate day in the league, was a lot worse: a tragedy narrowly avoided. The Euroborg was full to the brim. Groningen's fans for whatever reason cannot stand Ajax, as history has shown. The situation was made even worse as Suárez, Groningen's lead forward, had moved to Ajax the previous summer, and Ajax had 'stolen' Bruno Silva and midfielder Rasmus Lindgren during the winter transfer market. The *ultras* had prepared a little dance routine, South American style. When the two teams came on to the pitch for the warm-up, hundreds of toilet rolls were thrown on to the pitch. The stands behind the goals were covered in streams of loo roll. While the ground staff started to remove the paper, it caught fire. It was not clear whether the fire started by accident or on purpose. It spread literally like wildfire and started to burn the green seats. A toxic black and white smoke filled the stadium. The referee had no choice but to ask the two teams to return to the changing rooms while the fans from the two teams exited the stands. Several fans jumped over the glass protection separating the stands from the pitch, whereas others just covered their noses and mouths and stuck it out. The fire brigade had arrived and were putting out the fire. Chaos, panic and fear. Luckily no one was seriously injured. The toll was twenty injured – nineteen for having breathed the fumes and one for minor burns. The match was suspended, as it was not safe to play in such conditions, and was rescheduled for three days later on 16 April. Suárez was 'welcomed' to the pitch with a chorus of boos and whistles. Every touch of the Uruguayan player was met with the same booing and whistling. There were banners all round the stadium accusing Suárez of being a mercenary. Just to make sure it was clear, next to the Uruguayan flag was Suárez' name and the dollar sign. In the 65th minute, after various misses from Suárez, he scored from a cross. He held his head in his hands, covered his mouth and did not celebrate the goal. After the match at the press conference, Luis explained: 'I did it out of respect for the fans; I think it was the right thing to do.' The Amsterdammers won 2-1 ...

On 14 July 2008 at the De Thij Sportpark in De Lutte, the first training session of the 2008/09 season got under way. Lots of things had changed at the club. A multimillion-dollar spending spree had brought Miralem Sulejmani, Ismaïl Aissati, Darío Cvitanich, Evander Sno, Eyong Enoh and Oleguer to Ajax. These players were bought to bolster the weaker areas of the team so they could push for the Dutch league title, which they had not won for three seasons, and to get back into Europe. As of 1 July 2008, Marco van Basten, ex-Ajax and Milan star who won the Ballon d'Or three times and was Champion of Europe with Holland in 1988, had been appointed to manage the team. He had started his coaching career with the youth teams at Ajax in 2003; just one season before getting his teeth into the Dutch national team in 2004. He took the team to the last sixteen in the Germany World Cup where Holland were beaten by a strong Portuguese side. He also qualified the team for Euro 2008 but things did not work out in Austria and Switzerland. In the quarter-finals, Russia kicked the team in orange out of the competition in extra time. Van Basten decided it was time to go back to his roots. In February of that year, prior to the Euro defeat, he had signed a four-year contract with his beloved Ajax. That the *Cigno di Utrecht* (the Swan of Utrecht), one of the greatest and most graceful players of all time, with 300 goals to his name, would get along with a striker like Suárez seemed completely natural. And yet the two did not see eye to eye at all, their vision of the game was different. Van Basten tried to find the most useful position for Luis but in so doing moved him around too much. Luis was bamboozled by van Basten's creative approach to team bonding, whereby players would be invited to play volleyball or paint together to unite the team. Luis was confused. He thought he had come to Ajax to score goals, not to paint pictures. Suárez and van Basten barely talked. It was clear that the relationship was not working.

Gabriel Francisco García de la Torre, better known as Gabri, midfielder for Barcelona who arrived at Ajax in 2006, recalled the atmosphere as follows: 'I don't know, I think van Basten thought us Hispanic players were less disciplined, less attentive to the coach's orders; maybe it was our way of playing and being in a team. Also van Basten did not have a huge amount of experience as a manager of a club. Maybe Ajax was a bit too big for him at that time. He was not the right person at the right time. Basically my relationship with van Basten was complicated just as it was for Luis.'

Van Basten acknowledged that 'Suárez was an important player for the club; he took part in every attacking manoeuvre. He was unpredictable and this made him special.' However, van Basten was not a fan of his modus operandi: 'He did not do us any favours racking up so many fouls. The risk is that, if he continues like this, he will be sent off every other foul.'

Van Basten promised to speak to the Uruguayan star and encourage him to be more restrained on the pitch, saying that he would have to discipline him if that was what it would take. The idea was to master the beast within Suárez but this was easier said than done, especially as Suárez was scoring lots of goals and improving his moves.

Suárez ended the season with 22 goals in the league and 34 in total – just one goal fewer than the lead goal-scorer of the Eredivisie: Mounir El Hamdaoui at AZ Alkmaar.

He was also second in the list of the most cautioned player with seven yellow cards. The Ajax fans did not care, they loved him. They voted him Player of the Year. For them, *El Pistolero* was an idol. This nickname was given to him after he scored a goal and then pretended to pull out two pistols and blow the smoke off the top. The idea came to Suárez when he was chatting to Sofia and his brother Paolo; it was a popular gesture which had captured the imagination of the fans and journalists.

Lucho had the hacks in the palm of his hand and the fans too. Marco van Basten on the other hand left Ajax. On 6 May 2009 he handed in his letter of resignation because he had not managed to achieve the goals set when joining the club. He had not won the league or qualified for the Champions League. His view was that: 'I have worked well with the people at the club; what is not acceptable are the results for which I am totally responsible.' Van Basten felt he did not have the resources and the energy to put things right and with great regret he threw in the towel.

It was a throw-away season for van Basten but a stellar season for Suárez. Even off the pitch things were going swimmingly for him. Amsterdam, the city of a thousand canals, gave him great freedom; he could go shopping with Sofia without anyone stopping him for his autograph or a photo. Amid the tourists who crowded the streets of the 'Venice of the North', he slipped by unnoticed. The locals were much more reserved than the Uruguayans. Even those who did recognise him shook his hand or said hello but nothing more. There were no paparazzi hiding round every corner or outside his house, and the tabloids did not focus on him. He lived in the centre of town just one kilometre from the train station in a modern anthracite-coloured block with large windows. Ajax was a club that knew how to look after its young players: it gave him a house, a rental car and helped him with the thousands of problems that daily life throws at you. At Ajax he met a group of Hispanics who made him feel at home.

Gabri recalled: 'It was purely by chance but at that time there were five or six Hispanics – Spaniards, Uruguayans and Argentines. There was Oleguer and Roger [García Junyent] from Barcelona, Bruno Silva, Luque, Darío [Cvitanich] the Argentine and in January 2010 Nicolás Lodeiro arrived from Uruguay. We made up 20% of the team and even though we got on well with the Dutch players, we ended up socialising together. Our table in the canteen was the noisiest and loudest. There were lots of jokes, laughter and stories all told at the top of our voices. We often went out for dinner together. We always ended up at Mi Sueño, an Argentinian grill bar. It was our meeting point. The question we would always ask was where could we go to eat. We always ended up there because they knew us and always treated us well. We celebrated there after the civil ceremony between Sofia and Luis, and on birthdays as well.'

Necdet Kul, the owner of Mi Sueño, a Turk from Istanbul, wove his way around the tables dressed in traditional costume: *sombrero* and red *foulard* despite the stifling heat coming from the grills in the kitchen. When he finally got a spare moment to come and talk, he got straight to the point: 'I have met a lot of footballers but none like Luis. I admire him for his love of football, for the way he plays and for the fact that he is a gentle, kind person who is easy to get on with. He used to come here with his friends, with his teammates and Sofia was always there. What did he eat? Chorizo, empanadas, provolone, meat and a panqueque. With lots of *dulce de leche* [a type of crème caramel] to finish off.'

Gabri clarified: 'Apart from those meals out, Luis was not a night owl and did not like going out in the evening. He had a girlfriend and liked being with her. He was a serious kind of guy, mature for his age, he had clear ideas, he knew what he wanted and where he was headed.'

A serious young lad who on 15 July 2009 became the new captain of Ajax. Thomas Vermaelen, the previous man at the helm, had left for Arsenal. Martin Jol, the new manager, chose *El Pistolero* as the man to lead the team. The decision was announced to the team during the briefing before a friendly against Bristol City. Jol explained the decision as follows: 'Luis is one of the most important players in the team. He proved this last season. Both on and off the pitch, he has made a very good impression on me. I am very happy that he wants to stay at Ajax to grow as a footballer. I hope that also this year he can make an important contribution to the club.'

Suárez had already worn the black armband when Vermaelen was not playing in the 2008/09 season but this was the official recognition of his supremacy.

Ronald De Boer commented: 'Normally the captain is the goalkeeper, an experienced defender or a playmaker. With Suárez , you had no idea what to expect but he showed that he deserved the responsibility of wearing the black armband. He looked after the team and was a positive example for his teammates. If someone made a mistake, he comforted them. He would say, "Don't worry, next time you will do better."'

The black armband was good for Suárez. He became a more disciplined and more mature player. On top of that he was working with a new manager. Martin Jol was 53 years old when he signed the three-year contract with Ajax on 29 May 2009. He had played in midfield for ADO Den Haag, Bayern Munich, Twente, West Bromwich Albion and Coventry City. As a coach he has been to Holland (Roda JC), England (Tottenham) and Germany (Hamburg). He had experience, he knew how to talk to players and earn their trust, and more importantly he did not have a background with Ajax. He changed the classic Ajax formation of 4-3-3 to a more traditional 4-4-2 formation which left more room for Suárez. It gave him the freedom to move and convinced the entire team that their attacks should revolve around Suárez. *El Pistolero* returned the favour by scoring a load of goals. On the second day of the league, he scored a hat-trick. It was 8 August and Ajax were playing newly promoted RKC Waalwijk. The match was tough and at 31 minutes into the game, the score was 1-1. *El Salta* took the game by the scruff of the neck and put three in the back of the net: one penalty, one from a distance and a tap-in on top of the goal.

On 20 September, Suárez bettered himself. The four goals which led his team to victory against VVV Venlo were all his doing. And if that were not enough, Luis managed to do even better on the eve of Christmas Eve in the last sixteen match of the KNVB Beker, the Dutch Cup. It was 23 December and Ajax was playing WHC Wezep, an amateur team. It ended 14-1, which was a record for Ajax. Prior to that, the highest number of goals scored in a match was in 1961 (10-0 against Rapiditas Weesp). *El Pistolero* scored six goals (two in the first half and four in the second). It was a shame that the game was slightly marred by a yellow card he picked up, which meant he would miss the quarter-finals. At the end of 2009 Suárez had scored a total of 46 goals including international matches. He was nominated for best goal scorer of the year and entered the list of the fantasy league perfect team in the Eredivisie, where he was top of the league table with eighteen goals in seventeen matches.

Suárez' numbers were impressive and lots of clubs started to show their interest: German clubs such as Bayern Munich, English clubs such as Chelsea, Spanish clubs such as Barcelona and Italian clubs like AC Milan. Suárez had always said that one of his dreams was to play for a Spanish club. He told one Uruguayan newspaper why: 'It is a beautiful country where my partner's family live. It has a very competitive league which the whole world talks about. It is where the best in the world play.'

Luis was also fond of the Premier League but he was not 100% sure whether he could deal with the physical game in England. A lot of players have had their fingers burnt despite their potential and failed to realise their dreams. Luis decided to stay with Ajax for the time being. In order to avoid the usual rumours on the transfer market, in the January of 2009 he signed a contract which expired in 2011. A better salary and a secure position for two years.

The first three matches of 2010 were a wash-out for Suárez. He failed to score a single goal. At this point, his last goal was on 11 December. On 3 February against Roda JC, Suárez found his form again and scored four goals: two penalties and two during play. By March, the Ajax captain had bagged 26 goals in 25 matches and was the best goal-scorer in Europe. He was better than Rooney, who had scored 23 in 27 matches. If that was not enough, he had scored twelve goals in the Dutch Cup and in Europe.

Martin Jol (as *El Pistolero* would confess some time later) had made Luis feel important and it had made him a better football player. He had become a lethal weapon that never missed. His side-kick, the Serbian Marko Pantelić, worked well with Luis, unlike what happened with Huntelaar whose style was not compatible with Luis'. Pantelić and Suárez fed off each other. Ajax scored 106 goals at the end of the season and had only twenty goals against them: Ajax had the best attack and defence in the league. It missed out on the league title by one point. FC Twente pipped them to the post under the careful management of Steve McClaren, the ex-manager of the England team. It was Twente's first title.

Ajax washed the bitter taste out of its mouth when it managed to win the KNVB Beker (Dutch Cup) on 6 May 2010 against Feyenoord: 4-1 the final score. Suárez was playing and he had his goal-scoring boots on. He scored his first in the fourth minute and his second and the last goal of the match in the 84th minute. He pulled off his shirt to reveal a Uruguayan shirt with the colours of Nacional on it. It was party time. It was Suárez who picked up the Cup and held it to the sky as the paper confetti poured down around the stadium. He had been waiting a long time for this moment. It was his first European trophy and the fitting end to a fantastic season. 49 goals in 48 matches. 35 goals in the league over 34 matches. This equalled the record of a foreign goal-scorer in the Eredivisie held by Mateja Kežman, who in 2002/03 scored 35 goals for PSV Eindhoven. It was an achievement that gave Suárez, number 16, the title of lead goal-scorer for the Eredivisie, Player of the Year as voted by the Ajax fans, and Dutch Footballer of the Year awarded by *De Telegraaf* newspaper. He also achieved fifth place in the European Golden Boot. Suárez scored one more goal than the winner, Lionel Messi, but the points awarded, depending on which league the goals were scored in, penalised Suárez. Now that Suárez had reassured Ajax fans that he was staying because he wanted to play in the Champions League and take the club to greater heights, it was time to focus on the Uruguay international matches in the South African World Cup. With a baby on the way, they were exciting times for Suárez.

Chapter 11
Hand of the devil

Everyone in life wants to be remembered for something good they have done, for something good that they managed to achieve. The same goes for football. Every player wants someone to remember that goal, that match, that player who was the best …

No one wants to go down in history as the one who did something bad, committed a terrible foul or made a horrible gesture on the pitch. The *beau geste* is much more fitting, as the French say.

And yet sometimes a *beau geste* can be smothered by a single act. This is what happened to Luis Suárez in the 2010 South African World Cup. Luis would like to be remembered for the beautiful goal he scored against South Korea which, after 40 years, put Uruguay through to the quarter-finals. But for the South Africans and most spectators around the world, he will be remembered for the handball off the line against Ghana. Many commentators defined it as the 'hand of the devil'. This was what the South African *Sunday Times* ran with. On the front page of 4 July 2010, there was a picture of Suárez with a pair of horns on his head, bloodshot eyes and a mouth dripping with blood like Dracula or Lucifer. Suárez not only saw this but he kept a copy as a prize possession. He found it highly amusing. The hand incident on 2 July 2010 was the hand of God for Luis and Uruguay.

Three years and five months had passed since Suárez

started his international career with Uruguay. On 7 February 2007 in the General Santander stadium of Cúcuta, Uruguay played Colombia. It was a friendly in which Óscar Washington Tabárez could experiment and test the up and coming players. Lucho was up. He was just twenty years old. He entered the pitch with number 10 on his back. It was his moment. In the thirteenth minute, *El Salta* beat the line of defence and charged towards the Colombian goal, chasing after a long pass behind the defence which caught them by surprise. He cut into the area and was about to shoot but Miguel Calero, the Colombian goalkeeper, instead of blocking the ball, went for the striker's feet. Penalty. Calero was sent off. *El Loco* (the crazy one), Sebastián Abreu, converted the kick in the seventeenth minute. Another penalty for Abreu in the 60th minute took the score to 2-0. The match ended 3-1 to Uruguay but Lucho did not see the match out. In the 85th minute, referee Jorge Hernán Hoyos sent him off for a second yellow card. Suárez had been giving him too much lip for a decision he had made. The referee had had enough of the abuse and it was an early shower for Lucho.

After his debut match with Uruguay, the next commitment was the U20s World Cup in Canada. Suárez was asked to play. He had already been called up for the U20s South American Cup in Paraguay from 7 to 28 January. The tournament was won by Brazil, with Uruguay taking third place – thus qualifying the Light Blues for the World Cup. Edinson Cavani was the lead goal-scorer with seven goals. Luis was not there, however, as Groningen had not given their permission. He stayed in Holland but fortunately was allowed to partake in the U20 World Cup.

On 1 July 2007 in Burnaby, the third-largest city in British Columbia, the first match of the U20 Uruguay team was played. Gustavo Ferrín was the coach and the team had involved players like Mathías Cardacio, Martín Cáceres, Emiliano Alfaro and Tabaré Viúdez. Uruguay were up against Spain who were playing Gerard Piqué, Juan Mata, Diego Capel and Javi García. Suárez wore number 18 and was play-ing on the left behind Cavani, 9, the lead striker. In the 55th minute, Suárez received the ball outside the area and struck a missile which deflected off the crossbar and into the net. 'What a strike!' bellowed the Canadian TV commentator. It was 2-0 to Uruguay at this point (Cavani and Suárez one apiece). Spain clawed back with a strike from Adrián López and a goal from Capel in the dying seconds of the match.

Uruguay ended the first phase of the tournament in third place in Group B with one win (1-0 against Jordan), one loss (0-2 against Zambia) and the draw against Spain. Uruguay was lucky enough to make it through. In the last sixteen, they were up against the USA. Things were looking good and in the 73rd minute Cavani headed a cross and Brian Perk, the US goalie, fumbled it and Suárez slammed the ball in the back of the net. The USA came back with an own goal from Cardacio and in the 107th minute of extra time, the USA scored the winner: 2-1 the final score. The Yankees were through and the Uruguayans were not to make the final as they had in Malaysia in 1997.

Suárez' next appointment with the Light Blues was on 12 September 2007 at Ellis Park in Johannesburg: a friendly against South Africa. The Uruguay team were using the match as a warm-up for the 2010 World Cup qualifiers. The South Africans, coached by Carlos Parreira, saw it as a test for the Africa Cup of Nations, which was to be held in Ghana in 2008. The match was lifeless and ended 0-0. However, the match marked the moment when Suárez became a perman-ent member of Tabárez' national team.

His first goal with the number 9 shirt came in the Estadio

Centenario against Bolivia on 13 October 2007: the first qualifier of the Conmebol for the South African World Cup. It was the fourth minute of the match and Luis creamed the ball at the goal. The goalkeeper failed to hold it. Martín Lasarte, Luis' coach when he played for Nacional, was in the crowd and, even though he was not one for shouting, he let out a cry of joy when the ball hit the back of the net.

Suárez played nineteen of the twenty qualifiers for the 2010 World Cup. He scored against Chile, Venezuela, Colombia and Ecuador (in Quito). The goal he celebrated the most was the one in Quito, along with the one against Colombia. He had let himself and his coach down in the previous match. The goal lifted everybody's spirits. The last few matches of the qualifiers were not so kind to Suárez. He had lost his goal-scoring streak. Both with Ajax and Uruguay, his Midas touch just was not there. Tough times but Uruguay still made it through.

It was 18 November 2009. Luis was on the pitch celebrating, together with 60,000 fans in the Centenario stadium, the 1-1 draw against Costa Rica which was Uruguay's passport to the South African World Cup. Uruguay qualified in fifth place and needed the draw to get through. Uruguay had to make it after having not qualified for the Germany World Cup in 2006. The fans screamed at the top of their voices: 'Soy celeste, celeste soy' (I am light blue, light blue I am).

On 5 June 2010, the Light Blues landed at Johannesburg airport in South Africa. They were immediately whisked off to Kimberley, provincial capital of Northern Cape, a little town famous for the 1899 siege during the Second Boer War and also for its diamond mines. The Big Hole was the symbol of the past: a black hole, 240m deep and covering a surface area of 17 hectares. Between 1871 and 1914, around 50,000 miners extracted 2,722kg of diamonds.

In the GWK Stadium (home ground of Kimberley, the rugby team), the Uruguayans started to train and adapt to the South African climate. Uruguay were in a group which had been defined as the group of doom. They were up against France, recent World Cup runners-up, South Africa and Mexico, both of whom were tough cookies.

The first match was in Cape Town on 11 June against the French. The Blues had qualified in the South African World Cup against Ireland coached by Giovanni Trapattoni, thanks to a double Thierry Henry handball which had caused a huge scandal. It was more or less the same team that had lost on penalties in the final against Italy. Only the captain, Zinedine Zidane, the man who lost his rag against Marco Materazzi and headbutted the Italian defender, was out.

It was 8.30pm. France were in white, Uruguay in light blue on the Green Point Stadium pitch. Suárez, wearing number 9, was up front with Diego Forlán as part of a 4-4-2 formation which coach Tabárez had carefully selected. Suárez was substituted in the 27th minute of the second half by Loco Abreu.

Luis would be remembered for his knock-on to Forlán, despite pressure from Gallas, who skewered the ball wide.

There were few chances: a parry by Hugo Lloris from a Forlán bomber and the flick from Fernando Muslera off Yoan Gourcuff's free-kick. Nicolás Lodeiro was sent off for a mega foul on Sagna. There was nothing of note for the rest of the match. A 0-0 flatline draw. Neither team could come up with the goods. Tabárez confirmed what everyone thought by stating that he was happy with a point but not with the way the team played. The Uruguayan press went to town. Their team was not up to the challenge and looked dreary on the pitch.

The other Group A match, Mexico vs South Africa, ended in a draw. The damage was contained.

The second match with the South Africans was crucial. The losing team would almost certainly be packing their bags.

It was 16 June in Pretoria: the vuvuzelas provided the soundtrack to this do-or-die match. The Loftus Versfeld Stadium was a cacophony of monotones. Nelson Mandela's fatherland were hoping to repeat the success of the Springboks, the national rugby team which won the Rugby World Cup in 1995 and 2007. It was not their year. Uruguay shattered the dreams of an entire nation which had been preparing for this special tournament. Diego Forlán, sitting behind Cavani and Suárez, scored two goals which cleared the path for Uruguay. The first came after twenty minutes and it was a scorcher, an air-bender from 30 metres which looped and slotted under the bar. The second was a penalty. Khune, the South African goalkeeper, cropped Luis Suárez in the area. Khune protested violently to the referee, Massimo Busacca, but the Swiss referee was having none of it: Khune was sent off and the penalty kick was converted: 2-0. Álvaro Pereira wrapped things up for the Light Blues. A 30-metre Forlán pass to Suárez, which the number 9 controlled and crossed over the goalkeeper and the defence and Álvaro simply tapped in. Forlán was the best player on the pitch, Suárez was a tornado on the wing, so much so that the defender, Mokoena, had to stop him by resorting to unofficial tactics: an elbow in the face which left Suárez checking if all his teeth were still intact.

The South African fans left the stadium feeling moribund, their hopes and dreams of four years dashed.

Suárez kept pushing for a goal but he had to wait until 22 June in the last game of the group phase. In the 42nd minute against Mexico came the first goal for *El Salta* in a World Cup.

Palito Pereira got the ball back for Uruguay in their half, and he passed to Forlán in the centre circle. Forlán turned and assessed the layout of his team. In the blink of an eye, he passed to Cavani who had run up the right flank, whereas Suárez was getting into position on the left. A perfect cross from Edinson and Luis freed himself from his markers and with a clean header the ball careered into the back of the net: 1-0. It was a goal which would take Uruguay to the last sixteen.

Uruguay had seven points and topped their group, thus avoiding a battle against Argentina who had topped Group B. South Korea were up instead. Under the rain in Port Elizabeth, Suárez played the perfect match. In the eighth minute, after Park Chu-Young had missed for the Koreans, Suárez scored for 1-0. It was an opportunist's goal. A cross from Forlán. Jung Sung-Ryong, the South Korean goalkeeper, dived late, the ball landed on Lucho's right foot and he slotted it in. A gift but it was not enough. South Korea pulled level. Suárez got his head down and did the business. He received the ball on the edge of the area, perfect ball control, dart to the right to free himself from his markers and then a quick glance and boom – the ball screeched through the air and slammed into the opposite corner of the goal. It was the 80th minute and Suárez celebrated like a man possessed; he jumped over the photographers behind the goalmouth and then ran to hug the reserve players. Uruguay was the first team to qualify for the quarter-finals. It was the first time since 1970 when Ladislao Mazurkiewicz, Víctor Espárrago and Luis Cubilla got to the semi-final but were beaten by Pelé, Carlos Alberto, Rivelino and Tostão's Brazil.

2 July 2010, Johannesburg, Soccer City: Ghana–Uruguay. The Black Stars were the last team from Africa in the tournament. Africa pinned its fading hopes on the team. The *Daily Sun* had a full-page spread entitled 'We're all Ghana fans today'. The South Africans even created a neologism for the occasion: *Baghana Baghana,* a mix of *Bafana Bafana* and Ghana. In the tunnel leading out onto the pitch, Óscar Tabárez hugged and kissed each of his players one by one. No one could have imagined that this would be the most dramatic match of the World Cup. It was the match of the hand of God or the devil depending on your viewpoint.

Diego Lugano and John Mensah, the two captains, read an appeal against racism before the match. The two teams lined up on the centre line and behind was a large banner which read: 'Say no to racism'. Eighty-five thousand spectators and a fired up crowd supporting the men in red and yellow. After 120 minutes the match was a stalemate at 1-1. Muntari had put Ghana ahead but Forlán from a spot kick had drawn level for Uruguay. The referee, the Portuguese Olegário Benquerença, blew for a foul by Jorge Fucile on Adiyiah. The Uruguayans vehemently disputed the foul. Fucile did not even touch the Ghanaian player. The free-kick was given nonetheless. Pansil took the kick and the ball looped into the area. Chaos ensued, with headers and jostling and players bundled to the ground. The ball was tapped off the line and then Adiyiah headed for goal. Muslera was beaten and Suárez, who was the last man on the line, remembering the times when El Chango Suárez had put him in goal, somehow parried the ball with both hands. Suárez was sent off and stood on the sidelines with his shirt over his head. He could not watch. Gyan stepped up to the plate and looked down the barrel of destiny. He took a long run up – and the ball slammed into the crossbar. The Ghanaians could not believe it. The referee blew for the end of the match. At the entrance to the tunnel, Suárez chewed his shirt nervously and then screamed with joy. He ran down the tunnel like a madman. It was all down to penalties now. Forlán was the first of the Uruguayans to step up: he scored. Muslera managed to block the third and the fourth penalties. The Light Blues were ahead by one goal. It was Loco Abreu's turn to shoot. The number 13 lived up to his name and scooped the ball in the back of the net. Uruguay were in the semi-finals. Suárez and Loco were the heroes of the match.

Lucho joked afterwards: 'It was worth getting sent off. It was the parry of the World Cup, the best. It meant we could win the match. It was a complex and difficult match; we suffered until the very end but now the hand of God is mine.'

Milovan Rajevac, the Serbian coach of Ghana, did not see it the same way: 'What hand of God? That was the hand of the devil. What hero? Suárez is a vulgar cheat.'

Rajevac took the matter to FIFA, stating that 'after a scandal like this, the rules of the game should change. The referees should award goals and not give penalties.'

In Montevideo no one cared. Suárez was a hero. Uruguay were in the semis of the World Cup for the fifth time. It was one of the four best teams in the world and Plaza de la Independencia was teeming with people, despite the winter cold and the late hour.

Meanwhile, back in Africa and England, the critics were having a field day about Suárez' 'hand of God' and that gesture that had rocked the footballing world.

On 6 July 2010, Luis Suárez had to watch Uruguay play Holland from the stands of the Green Point Stadium of Cape Town. He watched Giovanni van Bronckhorst beat Muslera with a missile from 30 metres, off the post and into the net.

Suárez shouted at the referee who appeared to be rather lax in enforcing fouls. Forlán drew level and Suárez was on his feet jumping for joy. The second half was painful and Suárez lost his rag when his team threw away two easy chances. A few minutes later and Suárez was suffering as his team went two goals behind with Wesley Sneijder and Arjen Robben showing what they were made of. Maxi Pereira pulled one back for Uruguay in the 90th minute but it did not change the outcome: Uruguay were out of the 2010 World Cup. The euphoria and hopes of an entire nation were brutally curtailed in a few crucial minutes. The grieving began.

Holland were off to the final against Spain and Uruguay were in the third place decider against Germany. Holland would lose to Spain in the 116th minute with a goal from Andrés Iniesta. Uruguay would end up fourth with a soulless 3-2 loss to Germany's *Fussballnationalmannschaft*. Diego Forlán was voted FIFA's best player of the World Cup. Suárez was booed when he entered the pitch. His 'hand of the devil' had not been forgotten.

Two days later on 13 July the words 'Orgullo celeste' (Light Blue pride) appeared on the side of a bus which was paraded around Montevideo, celebrating the World Cup achievements. Uruguay was only fourth but it was no mean feat: 'Gracias Muchachos!' (thanks lads); 'Gracias celestes por regalarnos un sol y dejarnos soñar' (thanks Light Blues for giving us the sun and days to dream'; 'Un país está con ustedes' (Your country is with you); '3 millones un mismo sueño' (3 million, one dream) – this is what the banners were saying.

Bunting and banners were everywhere. The streets were packed despite the chilly weather. It was a slow and long pilgrimage up to the Palacio Legislativo. Pepe Mujica, the President, presented: 'We have never been so united …

Thanks to the team on behalf of the entire Uruguayan people.' These were his first words of his speech. Then came the national anthem with medals awarded and a show put on by Loco Abreu for good measure. Each player was presented and when it was Suárez' turn, Abreu said: 'That was something spectacular you did that will stand the test of time; it was criticised by those who do not understand football because those that do understand, know that Luis Suárez ...' – the crowd interrupted *El Loco* with an 'Olé' – 'is the hand of God, no, not the hand of God but the hand of Suárez.'

Chapter 12
Come on, you light blues

A conversation with Jaime Roos

A father and son met in South Africa. One from Montevideo and the other from Amsterdam. The father is a musician, the son a photographer. They were to meet each other at the 2010 World Cup. They wanted to tell the story of the World Cup through music and video. The product of their creative efforts was the documentary *3 millones: La aventura Celeste contada por los Roos* ('3 million: The Uruguayan adventure told by the Rooses [Yamandú and Jaime]'). It was a two-hour documentary about a group of players and their coach in South Africa. It was an intimate tale of life and football which showed the passion, the suffering and the happiness through the eyes of an entire nation.

The story began at Carrasco airport when the charter plane of the national team took off for Johannesburg and ended with the trip back with the Light Blue heroes. It was a film where a father and son become the eyes and hearts of three million Uruguayans.

Jaime Roos was the father, the musician, the composer, the singer and the writer of songs such as 'Durazno y Convención', 'Si me voy antes que vos', 'Amándote' and 'Cometa de la Farola' ('Peach and Convention', 'If I go before you', 'Loving you' and 'Comet of the lamppost'), dedicated to his team Defensor Sporting.

He arrived at the coffee bar of a hotel in Montevideo. Impossible not to notice his huge moustache, bald head and long hair. In the entrance hall, the to and fro of tourists from Brazil who had arrived by coach. The first floor provided a bit of quiet to talk about his adventure and about Suárez. Jaime kicked off:

'I met Luis in South Africa when we were filming the documentary. We lived in Kimberley, the headquarters of the national team. We were lucky enough to see him train every day. I have a good relationship with Diego Lugano and Diego Forlán going back to the South Korean World Cup. I did not know Luis that well. He seemed quite a reserved person to me, hard to strike up a conversation with. Everyone in the national team admired and respected him. Playing with the national team has helped Suárez a lot both personally and professionally. He was in a group whose members had respect for each other; there was discipline and happiness. It was a positive environment which coach Tabárez had built over several years. It was a different set-up to the South Korea and Japan World Cup where the team was angry and divided. In South Africa, the atmosphere was pleasant and positive. In my humble opinion, this enabled Suárez to grow, improve and play better than in his club matches. Without taking the good things out of his personality, it smoothed some of the rough edges. On the pitch he proved he was a top-class player. I named him Tiburón (Shark) and I saw that others were doing the same thing: Depredador (Predator) was a favourite.'

Let's talk about Tiburón's style and attributes.
'Suárez for me is the classic Uruguayan player – not even Rio Platean, he is a true Uruguayan player. When I saw him, I thought I was back in the 1960s looking at the great players of Peñarol like Luis Cubilla, a player who did what he

wanted with the ball. If you watch how he played, he runs like Suárez; the way he places his body to defend the ball and the way he sets up a move is identical. Luis is a mélange of the great players from the past, from Schiaffino onwards. He has the ability to become the greatest number 9 in our footballing history. If you go and watch the kids playing in a side alley, you can see the same moves as Suárez does. However, if you watch Cavani or Forlán, you can tell that they are modern players, European players. Yes, I am convinced Suárez has the skill, the knack and hunger; he is an old-fashioned player who does not conform to the automatised manoeuvres of modern football. When Forlán, who was a grand master in the 2010 World Cup, has the ball at his feet, he knows exactly what he has to do. He is a computer: he processes information incredibly quickly and decides on the best option between A, B or C in the blink of an eye. Suárez, however, finds answer Z which no one expects.'

Let's take a look at Suárez' journey in the national team and in the South African World Cup.
'There is only one word to describe it: spectacular. He was the best Uruguayan goal-scorer. He beat Diego Forlán and Héctor Scarone's record. Scarone was the 1920s Messi. The story goes that he could slip the ball through a keyhole. Suárez' story, what with the South African World Cup, the Copa America in 2011 and all the shenanigans in England (racism accusations and the infamous bite), has a literary element to it. There is drama and comedy but in the end good wins over evil.'

Let's get back to the 2010 World Cup.
'I would like to talk about the infamous hand because I was there and I saw the reaction of the African and English press.'

Please continue.

'For me it was normal to commit a foul to stop a goal. It was voluntary but a hand is better than a goalkeeper who goes in hard as the South African goalie did with Suárez; an elbow in the face and a kick in the shins, which was a deliberate move to put his opponent out of action. Any country which has a minimum of football culture will understand that what Suárez did was normal. What is not normal was the hand of Diego Maradona, the original "hand of God", or the double hand of Henry against Ireland which enabled France to qualify – two hands to score a goal, not to stop one. Those were real scandals. Suárez' hand was not a disgrace but was a last resort to give Uruguay a chance of getting through. This is what I tried to explain to the Africans who were angry and confused by his gesture. They said to me that I was saying this because nothing like this had happened to Uruguay. I replied that they did not know about the history of football and that is why they lost. We had exactly the same thing in the 1990 World Cup. Spain vs Uruguay. The Light Blues were playing in the Stadio Friuli in Udine and were dominating play. It was a corner to us and José Herrera jumped higher than everyone else and headed the ball. Zubizarreta was beaten but Francisco Villarroya pushed the ball off the line with his hand. He was not even sent off. Yellow card and penalty. Rubén Sosa went to take it and booted it into the heavens. We remember the missed penalty of a great champion like Sosa, not the hand of the Spanish player, and yet all the press can say is 'you cheat'. This is where our 120 years of footballing history make the difference. If I am honest, what surprised me the most was not the reaction of the African press but the English press who do understand football. If I am not mistaken, in the 1966 World Cup, a certain Jackie Charlton saved a goal with his hands ... intentionally. The

World Cup is full of episodes like this. This is why the press merry-go-round caught me by surprise a bit.'

Apart from that incident, how do you view Suárez' 2010 World Cup?
'Forlán was the best player of the tournament, even FIFA acknowledged it. He knew how to read the play like no other and played his number 10 role to perfection. He was a step above Suárez who, for the record, played brilliantly together with Lugano and Diego Pérez who were the backbone of the team. He was a striker who had found his wings and was spreading them wide to get ready to take off.'

Chapter 13

Bite and run

And that made 100. In just three years with Ajax, Luis Suárez scored a ton, which only seventeen players have achieved in the long history of the club. He overtook stars like Johan Cruyff, Dennis Bergkamp and Marco van Basten who all took longer to reach the target with the Amsterdammers. Only two foreign players have done it: Jari Litmanen, a Finn, and Stefan Pettersson, a Swede.

The 100th goal came like a juicy, ripe pear on 28 July 2010 in the qualifiers for the Champions League against PAOK. The Ajax captain opened the score with a bicycle kick which was off the wall. With his shoulders to the goal, after a ping-pong in the area, he positioned and steadied himself and launched himself at the ball, which whistled through the air and struck the back of the net. Goal! This could be the best goal he scored with the red and white shirts, the number one in his top ten. And even if he said that he did not pay attention to statistics and records, he had been pushing and waiting for this 100th goal. He had prepared for the moment and when he ran to the crowd to celebrate, he lifted up his shirt and the Dutch words for '100th goal' were sprawled across his chest on a T-shirt.

El Salta, the Ajax captain, was the leader on the pitch and in the changing rooms. His shirt, number 16, sold the most in the shops and was the most visible in the crowd of fans. His photo was in the entrance to the club museum.

He was an inspiration for the young players in the academy. Everyone wanted to be like him. He had managed to pick up a bit of Dutch, enough to communicate and understand the intricacies of Dutch football tactics. Even his TV interviews were pretty fluent. His teammates were still amazed that he went everywhere with his thermos flask with warm water. Lucho was amazed that the TV commentators did not shout when a goal was scored as they would in Uruguay. He did not understand the cold nature of the Dutch, especially in relation to something as passionate as football.

He was also amazed that kids in Holland had everything, unlike in Uruguay. Kids had powerful cars given to them as birthday presents when they reached eighteen. He could not understand why the Dutch ate so early (6.00pm), whereas he continued to eat at 9.30pm as he would have done in Uruguay. But he had fitted in and adapted to the Dutch way of life. He had grown up in Amsterdam and Ajax. He was at home. He liked the quietness and the organisation of the club and that he did not have to meet up for two days prior to a match (unlike in Uruguay). The fact that he could stay at home with Sofia right up to a couple of hours before an important match was amazing. He was smiling and life was smiling back for the 23 year-old. Professionally everything was in order. He was the lead goal-scorer for the previous season. He had the Midas touch. He had played a fantastic World Cup. Yep, things could not be better. Even the red card on 31 July 2010 in the Dutch Supercup, for his tackle on Cheick Ismaël Tioté, the centre midfielder from the Ivory Coast – and the fact that Ajax lost in the final against Twente – could not dampen his mood.

On a personal level, his first child was on the way. On 4 August, the eve of the birth of Delfina, Lucho played PAOK in the return leg of the Champions League qualifiers. A nightmare of a match which ended 3-3. He scored the goal for 1-1 and was pulled off after Martin Jol thought Suárez was injured, whereas he was only play-acting to waste time. The result got them through to the play-offs and luck was on their side.

Suárez was back in action in the league on 21 August after having sat out two matches following his red card in the Supercup final. Against Roda JC, he scored his first of the season. A week later away from home, he was in the De Graafshap, which usually panned out well for Lucho. This time was no different! He stuck three in the back of the net, which he would repeat on 8 October 2010 for Uruguay in a friendly against Indonesia, a makeshift team which managed to score one goal against the Light Blues' seven.

The Champions League was not going so well, though. Ajax were in the play-offs and had beaten Andriy Shevchenko's Dynamo Kiev and had qualified for the group phase. It was Suárez' dream to play in a European tournament and now it had come true. Unfortunately, Ajax were in a tough group: Real Madrid, Milan and Auxerre. Real Madrid cruised to a 2-0 win in the first match played at Santiago Bernabéu. Luis was not playing due to two yellow cards he had picked up. The match with Milan ended in a humdrum draw at home. The first victory came on 3 November against Auxerre at the Amsterdam Arena. Suárez got the clincher for 2-1.

Seven days later, at a gala with 900 guests, Ruud Gullit, ex-Milan and Holland player, and Martin Jol presented Suárez with the MVP Trophy and the most goals scored in a season trophy for the 2009/10 season. Luis dedicated the trophies to his beautiful daughter Delfina, born on 5 August. Luis was smitten with his new addition to the Suárez family. He would go and sit with Delfina every morning before she woke up, just to revel in the wonder of life.

On the pitch, however, Mr Suárez showed his other side. He was a tour de force but also OTT at times. In fact, it was in the peace and tranquillity of the Dutch countryside that the Mike Tyson in him, the cannibal, the vampire, burst out and erupted in all its glory. It was Saturday, 20 November 2010. At 10.30 in the evening, in the Amsterdam Arena, in a classic Ajax–PSV Eindhoven match, the sparks flew. It was tense, as Ajax wanted to win to reduce the gap to PSV, who were at the top of the table on 34 points to Ajax's 28. The two teams were at each other's throats. Matches were always a bit of a brawl between the two teams but this time it was particularly close to the cliff edge. Suárez had it in for Afellay, as he had dived without being touched; he had a dig at Jonathan Reis, the young Brazilian forward. Swear words were exchanged and the verbal abuse was constant. The worst was still to come. In the 92nd minute, Rasmus Lindgren was sent off for a foul on Afellay. On the pitch, the usual protests flared up. Pushing and shoving and rude gestures ensued between the players. Suárez was arguing with Otman Bakkal, the Moroccan forward for PSV. Tempers rose and Suárez reached boiling point: he threw himself at his opponent and bit him in the neck. The other players pulled them apart and the two protagonists told each other where to stick it. It was over in a flash but the TV cameras had zoomed in and picked up the moment. The replay showed what had happened as reported by the Dutch TV commentators: 'Yes, Suárez has bitten Bakkal! I have never seen anything like it. He has done a Mike Tyson!'

Bakkal was confused and pulled down his shirt to show the referee the teeth marks on his neck. Mr Björn Kuipers did not want to know about it and did not get involved. He did not pull out his red card and a few seconds later he blew for the end of the match. 0-0. It looked as though all their differences had been forgotten and Suárez and Bakkal joked and hugged each other. The two went off the pitch chatting about this and that. The press would not let it drop: 'What happened with Bakkal, Luis?' was the first question Lucho was faced with. He calmly replied: 'It was a moment of madness which I cannot explain. I lost it. I apologise and ask Otman to forgive me.' The press were not satisfied.

The next day *De Telegraaf* ran the headline: 'The cannibal of Ajax'. The paper requested the footballing federation to intervene and take measures against Suárez. Martin Jol defended his man as he had done on other occasions. He said it was a 'love bite' and that Luis was a good kid and was not the violent sort. He decided not to take the captain's armband off him. This decision was severely criticised. Jol's defence of his player did not have the desired effect and Ajax decided to fine and suspend Luis for two matches. The KNVB disciplinary committee went down on Luis even harder. A seven-match ban, including the two-match ban of his club.

Luis Suárez was able to play again on 8 December 2010 in the Champions League but his league return had to wait until 4 February 2011.

Herman Pinkster, part of the Ajax staff, was the man who was closest to Suárez in his three and a half years at the club. At a restaurant bar in De Toekomst, the training centre for the club, he recalled those moments and the personality of the ex-number 16: 'There are two Luises: the one on the pitch and the one off the pitch. Off the pitch, he is a quiet, reserved, pleasant guy. You just have to watch him when he is with Sofia or Delfina to realise what he is really like. On the pitch he transforms. He is nervous, tense, stressed and angry. It is as though these two people co-exist: Dr Jekyll and Mr Hyde. Why? Because he lives football with an intense passion.

He always wants to win, come what may. [Pointing to photos on the wall of all the Ajax teams in its history] At this club we have never experienced a player like him. His determination, his hunger for victory, his rage. We have had to adapt to him and he has had to adapt to us. He is hot-blooded and that blood sometimes goes to his head and makes him do things he later regrets. Just like the Bakkal bite. I would like to add that Luis, when he thinks he is right, he does not change his mind, but when he knows he has made a mistake, he feels sincerely sorry. As it was in this case. He apologised to everyone and accepted his punishment.'

Luis apologised in Dutch and Spanish to Bakkal and Ajax via a Facebook video posted on 2 December 2010: 'I made a mistake, but in that moment I was pumped, my heart rate was racing and sometimes you do not think before acting. I regret what I did, I am my worst critic. I know I normally do not react like this. Now I just want to get back to working hard for the team.'

This message convinced a large section of the fan base. Many sent messages of consolation but it did not convince the federation. Four days after his public apology, Luis lost the man who had made him into who he was and had trusted him with the responsibility of the team. Martin Jol resigned on 6 December 2010 after a draw with NEC Nijmegen. Ajax had not won a match for five games in a row. The team was fourth in the Eredivisie and was five points behind Twente and PSV who were dominating the league. In the Champions League, Real Madrid pounded the white and red team 4-0 in the Amsterdam Arena.

It was Frank de Boer's chance to try to turn things around for the Ajaxers.

Luis would only play one match under de Boer's reign. It was at San Siro against Milan on 8 December, the last match of Group G. Milan had already qualified for the knockout stage. Ajax were playing for a third place in the group in order to qualify for the UEFA Cup. Suárez was playing in the classic 4-3-3 formation. He was alongside Miralem Sulejmani and Siem de Jong. He played a strong match but had to come off injured in the 90th minute. De Boer was pleased with the score (2-0 to Ajax) and hoped that this was the trigger to get his players back on the road to believing in themselves and back to their winning ways. De Boer must have been a fortune-teller as Ajax won the league title on 15 May 2011 after a six-year dry spell.

Luis Suárez had left months ago. The match against Milan was his last appearance for the Ajaxers. On 11 December he flew to Uruguay to spend a few days' holiday at his home at Solymar, a residential area by the sea about 20km outside Montevideo. He then headed east for a few more days' holiday and then back to Sofia and his daughter for Christmas and New Year's Eve. He gave an interview to *Ovación*, a daily sports newspaper in Montevideo, while he was there to talk about 2010. Luis said that it had been a great year and full of emotions. Luis talked about his best moments – the World Cup, his awards, the birth of his daughter Delfina – and the less happy moments. The bite, for example: 'They are things which happen so quickly. Everyone saw the bite but not what was going on in the match. We had had a lot of altercations during the match. He had stamped on my feet. I was really angry and I kept saying to myself that I would contain my anger and not give him a kick but when I got near him, I just wanted to bite him so I did. I thought it had gone unnoticed because there was a bunch of players around me but the TV cameras caught it. I did not expect the backlash that followed.'

Suárez accepted that he had made a mistake – a captain

of a team cannot behave like this – but he was annoyed that the club had not defended him and that they had not fought the sanction from the Dutch federation.

On 2 January 2011 Suárez headed back to Amsterdam, but he wanted a different future. He wanted a change. Dutch football was limiting. He wanted to improve. He wanted to go to a team where he could play alongside the best players in the world so he could progress. He wanted to work with a coach who would help him clean up his game. He stated that his dream was the Spanish Liga. But it was not for him to decide; he knew that the market ebbs and flows according to marketing pressures more than by how talented a player is. He was convinced that the World Cup had helped him in terms of his image. His Dutch experience was over. A few weeks later, he was on his way.

On 28 January 2011, three days before the winter transfer window closed, Suárez changed clubs. He had signed for Liverpool. The Reds had won the battle between clubs like Barcelona, Manchester United, Milan and Real Madrid and after an offer of €15 million missed the mark, they got their man for €26.5 million. It was a five-and-a-half-year contract. For a few hours it was Liverpool's most expensive transfer – that was until they paid €41 million to Newcastle for Andy Carroll. They had made their money by selling Torres, *El Niño*, to Chelsea for €58.8 million. Suárez was Torres' replacement (even if Kenny Dalglish was to deny it). Lucho was the most expensive South American player for two years. He had beaten the €21 million that Atlético Madrid paid to Villareal for Diego Forlán. This would only be beaten by Cavani: €64 million for his transfer from Naples to PSG.

But how did things really pan out between Liverpool, Ajax and Suárez? David Endt, team manager for Ajax from 1997 to 2013, told the story: 'A preliminary agreement with the player had been signed way back, perhaps even before the famous biting incident. Luis knew he was leaving not for the biting incident. There was never any controversy around that incident. He did not just pack his bags and head off into the sunset over money. He is not a mercenary. He wanted to leave to improve. He had seen that the moment was right to take that next step in his career. He was attracted to the Liga, Barcelona above all other teams, but the Catalonians did not make an offer. Several clubs called for information about him, including several Italian clubs, like Naples, but nothing more. The Premier League appealed to him, especially the history of a club like Liverpool. Luis was an idealist and these things mattered. The only doubts he had were around the competitiveness of the Reds. Were they good enough? I believe he spoke at length with the club management. The person who convinced him was Kenny Dalglish, the Liverpool coach. He told him that with him and the other new arrivals they could take the team to great heights, back to where it belonged. Luis listened and obliged.'

Luis left Ajax with 111 goals over 159 official matches. He left them with memories of his character, his style of play and his passion for football. He was an anarchist planted in an ordered field of Dutch tulips. Tom Egbers, a leading Dutch sports journalist, commented on the era as follows: 'He is one of the most spectacular players that Ajax has ever witnessed over its 100-year history. There is Cruyff, van Basten and then there is Suárez.'

In the Amsterdam Arena, Luis appeared one last time on 20 February. It was his final salute to the fans. He ran on to the pitch to a fanfare and a line of honour which the players had formed to show respect to their ex-captain. The banners around the stadium read 'Thanks Suárez' and the songs 'Volare' and 'You'll Never Walk Alone' boomed around the stadium. The maxiscreen showed his goals and the moves that had entertained the club over so many matches. Suárez thanked his fans and did a lap of honour of the pitch, kicking balls into the stands. The fireworks went off. It felt more like a welcoming ceremony than a farewell salute. It was impressive and emotional. *El Pistolero* was now a Liverpudlian. He was the Reds' number 7 – he had asked for it without understanding the history behind that magic number.

When he realised what that number meant for the Reds – that the poets of Liverpudlian football had worn it, from Kevin Keegan to Kenny Dalglish – he felt honoured. He promised Dalglish that he would make him proud and that he would not disappoint.

Luis made his debut as the number 7 on 2 February against Stoke City at Anfield Road. He came on in the eighteenth minute of the second half for Fabio Aurelio. Fifteen minutes later and he had scored. A long ball from Dirk Kuyt and Suárez ran on to it and skimmed past Asmir Begović, the Stoke goalie, and launched the ball towards goal. Wilkinson in a last-ditch effort to stop the goal tried to clear it, but he ended up hitting it into the post and the ball deflected back into the goal. It was the 79th minute and *El Pistolero* had shown the sceptics, those who had said he had come from a league which was too easy, that he was the real deal. His numbers for the first half of the season were not great: four goals in thirteen matches, including a magical goal from a corner against Sunderland. He did not play in the UEFA Cup but he showed his potential in matches against Manchester United and Fulham. He helped Liverpool move from twelfth place in the league to sixth at the end of the season. It was not ideal. C+, could do better.

Chapter 14
The best

In the Football Museum at the Estadio Centenario, it is there, just past the entrance. Next to the ticket office, in front of the stairs which take the visitor to the glory of the past, to when Uruguay's footballing history started and to the Olympics of 1924 and 1928 and the World Cup of 1930. To the right are the modern times. Next to Diego Forlán, best player of the 2010 World Cup, is a large photograph of a man with predator's teeth who is beaming at every visitor that goes past: Luis Suárez, FIFA's best player of the 2011 Copa America. It is a fitting homage to the number 9 who was key to Uruguay's fifteenth win of the continental tournament. The first tournament was played in 1916 in Buenos Aires, to celebrate the centenary of Argentina's declaration of independence. Uruguay won the tournament with Argentina second, a slur on Argentina's record which would be repeated in 2011 when Uruguay kicked the Argentines out of the Cup and then went on to win it, taking their tally to fifteen, one more than Argentina.

A Maracanazo but on a smaller scale. It was unforgettable for the citizens of the Eastern Republic.

Santa Fe, 16 July 2011. Brigadier General Estanislao López Stadium. Penalties. The goalkeeper went right and the ball went left. Leo Messi, the Argentine number 10, did not falter. It was the first of a series of five penalties.

Diego Forlán: Goal. Central and powerful.

Urreta FC with Luis front row, third from left.

Fast forward to 2006 and Suárez celebrates scoring for Nacional in his first season as a professional.

His early days at Groningen were a frustrating time for Suárez but a match-winning performance against Vitesse in October 2006 was the turning point, after which he never looked back.

In action for Ajax during the 2009/10 campaign. Suárez would finish the season as the league's top scorer and Dutch Footballer of the Year.

Dennis F. Beek/VI Images

Broer van den Boom/VI Images

Luis with his wife Sofia. Having a stable family life has been key to his success, especially during the difficult moments of his career.

Suárez' time at Liverpool was typically controversial but he would leave as the Premier League Golden Boot winner, PFA Player of the Year and FWA Footballer of the Year after a phenomenal 2013/14.

Suárez and Giorgio Chiellini after the infamous bite at Brazil 2014. The fallout from the incident saw Suárez sent home from the competition and banned from all football-related activities for four months.
AP Photo/Ricardo Mazalan

Suárez celebrates with his Barcelona teammates and the Champions League trophy after beating Juventus 3-1 in the 2015 final.

Nicolás Burdisso: Mid-height. Goal. Fernando Muslera guessed correctly but could not reach it. Goal.

Luis Suárez: He knew where he had to hit it. He did not look the goalkeeper in the face. Perfect strike to the right. Sergio Romero dived right but got there late. Goal! Kiss to the wrist and index finger pointed to the fans.

Carlos Tévez, the Apache: Short and fast run up. To the right of Muslera at mid-height but *El Nene* saved it. The Argentine number 11, the people's player distraught and in disbelief. Another mistake to add to the logbook.

Andrés Scotti and Walter Gargano slotted the ball in, as did Javier Pastore and Gonzalo Higuaín.

It was up to Martín Cáceres to take the final shot. Muslera was on his knees, praying and looking to the sky. The other Uruguayan players were huddled in the centre of the pitch. Gooooaal! Golazo! Muslera was the first to hug him and then there was a pile-on. Argentina were out and Uruguay was on its way.

The quarter-finals were tough and ended 1-1 after extra time (Pérez in the fifth minute of the first half and Higuaín at the seventeenth minute). Uruguay were playing with ten men as Diego Pérez was sent off for a foul on Higuaín. But Uruguay did not give up and they felt like they had the upper hand. They put their sweat, blood and tears into the match. They continued to fight and hold on to the ball. Suárez was a leading light: he defended like a man possessed (committing thirteen fouls), he chased down every ball and he was party to every Uruguay attack and counter-attack. After 120 minutes, he was exhausted but composed enough to be able to take the third penalty. He was in enemy territory and he finally achieved what he was looking for. He commented on his feelings at the end of the match: 'It is a great joy, I dedicate this success to the people of Uruguay and to those who have followed us from beginning to end at great cost.'

Uruguay needed it because the early stages of the tournament in Group C did not go exactly according to plan. In the first match against Peru on 4 July at San Juan in the Estadio del Bicentenario, Uruguay were down by one goal. Pablo Guerrero, the number 9 for Peru, was picked out with a long ball from midfield. He controlled the ball and skipped past Muslera, who was coming out, and slotted it into the open goal. Diego Lugano could not get there in time to keep it out: 1-0.

Uruguay reacted timidly. The Peruvians clamped down the midfield and cut off the lifeline between the defence and attack. Suárez was needed.

A good pass from Lodeiro to Lucho, and *El Salta* did not need to be asked twice: 1-1.

In the other two matches of the group stage, Suárez did not score. His involvement was fundamental, however: he was always a threat and causing problems for the opposition defence. His speed, agility and his desire to catch the defence on the back foot was inexhaustible. Uruguay was faltering, though: Chile was a draw and that meant that the match against Mexico would be decisive. If Uruguay won, they would be up against Argentina in the quarter-finals. When Suárez was quizzed about the potential match-up, he simply replied that the important thing was to qualify, and he quipped at the end in Obdulio Varela style: 'If we want to be champions, we have to beat any team. It is eleven against eleven on the pitch.'

Mexico tried their best at La Plata but there was no comparison. Mexico danced to the Uruguayan tune. Diego Forlán was the boss and Suárez was the move-maker. It ended with a respectable victory (1-0, Pereira) which meant that

Chile were first in the group and Uruguay second. Peru was third and would qualify.

Tabárez was at a turning point. It was the match of all matches against Argentina. Luis described the match as the hardest the two teams had ever played. Not just for the fact that it was decided on penalties but because both teams played their hearts out and Uruguay had taken the game to the Argentinians and made them play. Luis commented: 'Uruguay has shown it is well organised, keen to win and has *garra charrúa* [Charruan tenacity]. The team's dedication and enormous sacrifice was fundamental.'

It was from that evening, that cold evening in Santa Fe, that the Light Blues believed they could win the Copa America. The semi-final against Peru was an exhibition match for Suárez: he scored both the winning goals. The first half was tight, with Peru locking down the opposition team. Uruguay was countering but was not clear or lucid in attack. It was in the 53rd minute that the stalemate was broken. The reward for this breakthrough was the most beautiful cup in the world. Without Forlán and Suárez this would not have been possible. The Uruguay number 10 let rip a missile from 20 metres out. Raúl Fernández, the Peruvian goalkeeper, could not hold it. The ball fell to Suárez, who pounced on it like a savage wolf and kicked it into the back of the net between the post and the last defender. Four minutes later *El Pistolero* did it again. A quick one-two between Forlán and Álvaro Pereira on the left. A long ball from Palito cutting across the field. Luisito was in the right place between the two central defenders. He skinned the goalkeeper and from the edge of the area, put the ball in the goal. Forlán was euphoric and hugged Suárez for his superb effort.

It was 24 July 2011 in the Estadio Monumental in Buenos

Aires and Uruguay were playing the 21st final of the Copa America. The last Cup final the Uruguayans had played was twelve years earlier when they lost to Brazil. Their last win was in 1995 when they won on penalties against Brazil in the Estadio Centenario. This time it was Paraguay coached by Gerardo Tata Martino. Uruguay put out a strong team: Fernando Muslera, Maximiliano Pereira, Diego Lugano, Sebastián Coates, Martín Cáceres, Álvaro González, Diego Pérez, Egidio Arévalo Ríos, Álvaro Pereira, Diego Forlán and Luis Suárez. The first moments were appalling for the Paraguay side and a complete write-off. Within a couple of minutes Suárez was in their area and fighting for the ball with two defenders; he managed to free himself, get off the ground and shoot. The next corner, Justo Villar saved a header from Lugano and another from Coates which was pushed off the line by Néstor Ortizoga. The handball was clear for all to see. The Uruguayans demanded a penalty but Silvio Fagundes, the Brazilian referee, claimed not to have seen anything untoward. The goal came in the eleventh minute from a long ball from *Ruso* Pérez. Luis darted into the area, switched and sold the defender a dummy and pinged the ball against the post and in: 1-0. *El Pistolero* shot his Colts into the crowd before diving on the pitch and being smothered by his teammates. The crowd went wild and chanted: 'Suárez, Suárez'.

Forlán decided to join the goal-scoring party after a dry spell in which he had failed to score for over a year for the Uruguayan team. Arévalo Ríos stole the ball from Ortizoga and played an assist to the number 10. Diego struck the ball and goal number two was on the scoreboard. It was Diego who closed out the goal-scoring with a great effort in the 89th minute: counter-attack, Suárez assist and goal number three. Uruguay were champions of America. Forlán added another chapter to the family history book. He had won the title that his father, Paolo, won in 1967 as a player and his grandfather, J.C. Corazzo, won in 1959 as coach. Luisito won another title as well. FIFA awarded him player of the tournament. Photos, parties and the joy of an entire nation filled the Buenos Aires streets.

Chapter 15
'Negro'

It was the 58th minute, on the edge of the Manchester United penalty area at the Kop end. Suárez fouled Evra. Luis knocked Evra's right knee voluntarily. It was a clear foul. The referee blew for a free-kick. Evra laid on the floor for a minute and was tended to by the medical team.

At 62 minutes and 37 seconds, Suárez won a corner for Liverpool. He collected the ball from behind the net, kicked it to Steven Gerrard and headed off to the centre of the box. Evra, his marker, moved towards him. Words flew and the two were arguing almost in the goal. Evra started the high-brow debate with '*la concha de tu hermana*' (your sister's pussy). Suárez pretended not to have heard Evra's soliloquy. Suárez: 'What was that?' Evra retorted: 'Why did you kick me?' Suárez's alleged response, according to Evra, was: 'Because you are black.' (Suárez denied this and stated that all he said was that it was a typical foul.) Evra replied: 'Say that again and I will hurt you.' Suárez, according to Evra's witness statement, politely replied: 'I do not talk to blacks.'

The Uruguayan star would categorically deny the French defender's allegations. Suárez stated that all he said was that Evra should shut up and that he imitated someone talking by making a 'quack, quack' gesture with his hand to express his opinion that Evra was talking too much.

Evra was not done with the pleasantries: 'I am going to

hurt you for real.' According to Evra, Suárez touched his arm, pointing to the colour of his skin, and replied: 'OK, *blackie, blackie, blackie.*'

63 minutes and 5 seconds, the corner was taken. Suárez, marked by Evra, ran to the ball and flicked it on with his head. Andre Marriner, the referee, blew his whistle and stopped the game. The linesman informed the referee over the radio that something was going on between Suárez and Evra. The referee called them over to calm things down. Evra said to Suárez: 'Don't touch me, South American.'

Suárez: 'Why, *negro?*' Suárez would later claim that he had used the word '*negro*' as it is used in Uruguay, i.e. as a sign of friendship or when referring to someone who is black- or brown-skinned or just black-haired. It was not a racial slur. It was how he called his teammate, Glen Johnson. He had never intended using the term '*negro*' to racially offend or insult. He was merely trying to sort things out with the French defender.

Marriner, who had been refereeing a fairly event-free match up to that point, did not want things to get out of hand. He called the two over, asked them to calm down and to apologise to each other. Marriner claimed that he did not hear Evra who, when walking over to Marriner, said: 'Ref, ref, he just called me a f***ing black.'

Marriner gave Evra and Suárez a lecture and then sent the two away. Suárez placed his hand on Evra's head, which Suárez claimed was a friendly, peace-making gesture. Evra did not see it like that and pushed Suárez away. Marriner saw what was going on and called them back. He told Suárez not to touch Evra. He spoke to Evra and then the game restarted. Evra and Suárez exchanged words as they walked off.

This was the summary of the Football Association of those four minutes, which would cost Luis Suárez an eight-match ban and a £40,000 fine. The document was published on 31 December 2011. In the 115-page document, which explained the reasons for the fine, the events were set out with the witness statements of those involved, including the referee, and the TV images.

The Liverpool–Manchester United match on 15 October 2011 would keep the press, clubs and fans occupied for months. France, England and South America debated these racist acts.

Patrice Evra, the Senegalese player with a French passport, at the end of the 1-1 match, went back to the changing rooms and vented his spleen with his teammates.

He told his version of events and Suárez' alleged racist comments. Antonio Valencia and Anderson Luis de Abreu Oliveira convinced him to talk to Sir Alex Ferguson, the Man U coach. They told him to speak to the referee because it was a serious incident. This was exactly what the coach and the number 3 did. Andre Marriner listened to the statements of the player and added them to his match report. Marriner made Liverpool aware of the claim. Kenny Dalglish, the Reds' coach, went to Marriner to explain what he thought had happened according to Suárez. He said Suárez was not present because he did not speak English very well. Dalglish's statements were added to the report.

At the end of the match, Patrice Evra gave an interview to Canal+. Stéphane Guy, the French TV journalist, asked him if it was the first time that something like this had happened. Evra replied: 'Yes, it is the first time. The first time a player has said something like that to me, racist things. I am shocked because things like this in 2011 should not be said. Suárez did not need to do it. He wanted to get under my skin and upset me. If those sorts of insults come from the fans, it is still not acceptable, but from a player who you are up against, it is even harder to accept. Especially when you consider that he has played with players who have the same colour of skin as me. I do not want to blow this out of proportion but there will be an enquiry; there is a video where you can clearly read Suárez' lips and what he said to me. I will not repeat it but it was a racist insult and he repeated it at least ten times.'

Luis Suárez answered the claims on his Facebook page: 'I am mortified by the accusations of racism. I can only say that I have respected and respect everyone. We are all the same. I go on the pitch with the passion of a child, not to create conflict.'

Liverpool believed him, supported him and fought the allegations, claiming they were groundless. It should not be forgotten that the left back for Manchester United had accused a member of the Chelsea staff of racial abuse in 2008. The enquiry proved that the accusations were groundless. Evra was fined £15,000 and given a four-match ban. This time things would pan out differently. The FA started an enquiry and appointed an independent commission. On 16 November 2011, the FA charged Suárez with misconduct contrary to FA Rule E3 in relation to the Liverpool FC vs Manchester United FC fixture on 15 October 2011. The ruling was announced on 20 December.

Suárez, by now, was in the middle of another media tornado. This time Suárez was involved in offensive gesticulating. The incident happened at Craven Cottage in London. On 5 December, in a match against Fulham (who were coached by his ex-Ajax coach, Martin Jol), *El Pistolero* was photographed gesticulating to local fans. In short, he was giving them the bird. The gesture was a reaction to the fans' chants of 'cheat, cheat'. Kenny Dalglish stated that he had not seen the images and therefore had nothing to say.

The disciplinary investigation which the FA started ended with no further action.

The same could not be said for the Evra incident. Suárez was found guilty of misconduct, regarding 'using insulting words' against Patrice Evra of Manchester United. The insulting words used by Suárez included a reference to Evra's colour. The punishment of an eight-match ban and £40,000 fine were suspended while Liverpool decided whether to appeal against the ruling. This ruling had set a new precedent. Suárez was also banned from using racially offensive language, otherwise he would risk severe sanctions.

El Pistolero was shocked and surprised by the ruling. His lawyer, Alejandro Balbi, stated: 'He has taken this very badly but his family, friends, teammates, fans, Steven Gerrard the captain, and his club are with him.' Liverpool sided with Suárez. He was surprised and disappointed that the FA had given such a ruling solely on the allegations of Evra, which had not been confirmed by other players or by the referee or linesmen. Liverpool reiterated Evra's statement: 'I do not think Suárez is a racist.' A statement which the Football Association accepted.

Liverpool Football Club stated that the accusations against its player were dubious at best. They continued to defend him. They argued: Suárez is from a mixed-race background. His grandfather was black. He is personally involved in a charity project which promotes solidarity between mixed-race communities and people from different backgrounds and places emphasis on the fact that the colour of your skin does not matter. He has played with coloured players at Nacional and Uruguay and he was captain of Ajax, a club which is proud of its multi-race heritage.

The debate over the FA's ruling was fierce. The defence would explain time and again that '*negro*' and '*negrito*' in

South America is not an insult but a term of affection. They even resorted to seeking advice from expert linguists to explain the origins and meaning in Spanish.

Lila Píriz, Luis' grandma, told British tabloid *The Sun*: 'It is all my fault, I have always called him "*mi negrito*" right from when he was a baby.'

Liverpool continued to support Suárez unconditionally. During warm-up on 21 December before a match against Wigan, all of the team, including Dalglish, wore a T-shirt with his name, the number 7 and his face on it. The Reds' fans applauded this show of support vehemently; Wigan's supporters, on the other hand, whistled disapprovingly. The Liverpool fans talked of a witch-hunt. There was a statement from the team which said: 'We support Luis. We know he is not a racist.'

And yet, on 3 January, after having digested the FA 115-page report, Liverpool decided not to appeal against the ruling. They decided that continuing to fight the claim could have negative consequences for the fight against racism and further damage Liverpool FC's image. It was better to let it lie and close the case once and for all.

Luis came back to the pitch for the Reds on 6 February 2012. The second match after his ban was against Manchester United at Old Trafford. Everyone was waiting to see how he would react. The French and English pundits were debating on the correct thing to do: 1) bite him; 2) kiss him on the lips; 3) pretend nothing had happened; 4) ask for his forgiveness on one knee, etc., etc.

What actually happened no one could have expected, and it gave new life to the controversy surrounding the incident. In the pre-match ritual of shaking hands, Suárez shook everyone's hand except Evra's. He moved straight past Evra's held-out hand. At the end of the match, Evra went to celebrate Manchester United's 2-1 victory right under the nose of Suárez. The referee intervened to stop Luis from reacting.

Sir Alex Ferguson commented: 'He [Evra] shouldn't have done it.' However, he criticised Suárez: 'I could not believe Suárez refused to shake hands with Evra. Suárez is a disgrace to Liverpool. He should not be allowed to play for Liverpool again or be part of a great club. He could have caused a riot. It was terrible starting the match like that. Racism is an important issue and English football has come a long way since the days when they used to throw bananas at John Barnes, but we always need to be on the look-out.'

Kenny Dalglish was furious with the journalists' questions: 'I think you are bang out of order to blame Suárez for anything that happened here today.' Ian Ayre, sports manager for Liverpool FC, Standard Chartered bank, the £20m shirt sponsor for the club, and Fenway Sports Group, the American owners of the club, made it clear: Suárez' attitude was not acceptable. Luis' apologies were quick to follow: 'I should have shaken Patrice Evra's hand. I apologise for my behaviour. I want to leave this incident behind me and concentrate on my football.'

It would not be that easy, considering that the incident had become political. The Minister for Sport announced that David Cameron, the Prime Minister, would meet with the representatives of the world of football to prevent racism spreading in football as had happened in the past. The Minister insisted the FA take the shaking of hands incident into consideration. In Uruguay, South America and the Netherlands, the reaction was slightly different.

Héctor Lescano, Minister for Sport and Tourism in the Eastern Republic, had already gone on record offering his support for Suárez: 'I do not justify an act of discrimination, what I do say is that none of these accusations change the view I have of a kid who has always shown the utmost respect and affection.' *El Pistolero* was praised from various quarters. In his radio programme, *Habla el presidente*, on AM24, on 16 February 2012, Pepe Mujica started by saying: 'It is necessary that Suárez feels the affection that this small but big Uruguay has for him.' He insisted that Suárez was not a racist and he never will be. In referring to the hand-shaking incident, he added: 'Some people do not understand that Suárez did not study how to become a diplomat.'

Diego Lugano, the Uruguay captain, told it how it was: 'You need to have balls. He was completely honest with himself in front of a person (Evra) who had made him go through difficult times.' Óscar Washington Tabárez, who had not given an opinion on the incident, commented on *Radio El Espectador*. 'There are people whose hand I would not shake but I do not consider myself a bad person for this'.

And that was not all. In the Uruguayan afternoon in Amsterdam, the fans of Ajax, who were playing Manchester United in the UEFA Cup, did not stop chanting Suárez' name. In the evening, at the Parque Central in Montevideo, the support for Suárez was clear. Nacional had asked their fans to support Luis. The response was huge: in the Copa Libertadores against Paraguay's Libertad, hundreds of Suárez masks appeared holding banners which read: 'Ferguson, wash your mouth before speaking about Sir Luis Suárez'; 'Say no to the hypocrisy'; 'Suárez Uruguay is with you'. On the pitch, the players lined up behind a banner which read: 'Come on Luis'.

All there was left for Suárez to do was post a photo of him and Sofia on Facebook with the message: 'I want to thank all the fans of Liverpool for their support over the last few days. It has been incredible. With their permission, I want to thank Ajax fans for what they did today. As everyone knows, I am Uruguayan and I uphold the national team but I want to thank the Nacional fans, team and management for their support today!!! A big thank you to all of you!!!'

The controversy was not over. John Terry, the Chelsea defender and England team captain, was accused of racially abusing Anton Ferdinand in the Chelsea vs QPR match on 23 October, an incident which would lead to the resignation of Fabio Capello from the national team coach position and the end of John Terry's England career. But the ruling from the FA came almost a year after the event and the punishment was a lot less severe: a four-match ban and a fine of £22,000. The South American TV stations and newspapers saw the weaker punishment as a discrimination against Suárez.

Fortunately for Suárez and Liverpool, the media started talking about football again. On 26 February 2012, with *El Salta* on the pitch, Liverpool were playing Cardiff in the Carling Cup at Wembley Stadium. 2-2 after extra time. The Reds won on penalties and took their first title after six years of drought. The Reds won 5-3 in the shoot-out thanks to Anthony Gerrard (Steven's cousin) missing his penalty, the final one.

At the end of the season, Suárez had scored seventeen goals in 39 matches notwithstanding the eight-match ban. With eleven goals in the Premier League he was the lead goal-scorer in the team. The last goal of his hat-trick against Norwich at Carrow Road on 28 April was particularly impressive. He blasted the ball into the air from 45 metres after having seen that the opposition's goalkeeper was off his line. What a goal! The TV commentators went mad. The Reds' fans were over the moon. Suárez also gave Liverpool victory against Everton and qualified the Reds for the FA Cup final. It was a shame that on 5 May against Roberto Di Matteo's Chelsea there was nothing they could do. Ramires and Drogba silenced the Reds. On the last day of the Premier League, 13 May, Liverpool were playing away from home against Swansea and lost: 1-0. Liverpool finished the season in eighth place, 37 points behind winners Manchester City, coached by Roberto Mancini. A disappointing result which meant the Reds did not qualify for the Champions League. The result led Fenway Sports Group to back a different horse. On 16 May, Kenny Dalglish was sacked. He was criticised for his poor results and his purchase of the English trio of Andy Carroll, Jordan Henderson and Stewart Downing, which cost the club the tidy sum of £70m. There were no doubts about the sum paid for Suárez, which, leaving the controversy to one side, was a good investment.

On 26 July 2012, the 30th Olympic Games football tournament got under way. *El Pistolero* at 25 years of age was one of the three mature stars called to duty by Tabárez. The dream was to repeat the 1924 and 1928 successes. It was not to be. The Centenary Stadium would not be able to name one of its stands after the London Olympics as it had done with the Colombes and Amsterdam stands. The Light Blues were knocked out by England (1-0) on 1 August in the Millennium Stadium in Cardiff. The goal came from Daniel Sturridge, who a year later would move to Liverpool and team up with Suárez in attack. Uruguay were not convincing. There were too many holes in the defence and not enough grit in the attack. Luis gave his all but did not manage to score a goal in all three matches.

A few days after being knocked out of the Olympics, Suárez started training again with Liverpool. On the first day of training, 7 August, the Uruguayan signed a new contract with the Reds. The American owners shut every door in the face of offers from Juventus, PSG and other European clubs. Brendan Rodgers, the new Liverpool manager who took over from Dalglish on 1 June, stated: 'I am extremely happy he has signed a long-term contract with the club. I am happy as a coach as he is one of the best forwards in the world and I am happy for the players as I know what he means to them.' Luis was happy too. He confirmed that he was happy at the club. The fans were great, and he recalled how five or six years ago he saw Liverpool on the telly or played FIFA on the PlayStation with Gerrard and Torres and now he was one of them.

It looked like the Evra incident was behind him, but for some reason Luis just could not metabolise it and let it go. The club had told him not to mention it any more, but he could not stop talking about it. He told the press that he had not refused to shake Evra's hand. He talked about Manchester United's power and manipulation of the English media. In August, in an interview with *The Guardian*, he admitted he had felt he was a target following the racism accusations. He felt people had talked about the issue for the sake of talking about it without really knowing what went on. He said that he was not offended by the boos of the English crowds but that at the Olympics, when they booed the Uruguayan national anthem, that was a step too far. Two years later, Luis would admit to Sport 890, a Uruguayan radio channel: 'In my sporting career, I have made two mistakes, one in Ajax and one at Liverpool, against Ivanović. But regarding Evra, it was mostly made up as opposed to what really went down. They accused me without the proof.'

He told English magazine *Four Four Two*: 'I know that I was not and am not a racist. I have never said anything racist to him or any other football player.'

Chapter 16

A cannibal at Anfield

How do you ruin a fantastic season, full of goals, applause and happiness? Bite someone on the pitch. This was exactly what Suárez did. Everything was going swimmingly when it was as though Luis had forgotten the controversy surrounding the Evra incident and wanted to re-open the 'bad boy' debate with his critics. Luis was about to do something that would see him punished and his image tarnished yet again: the same mistake that had cost him a seven-match ban in Holland.

Up until 21 April 2013, there had been months of entertainment and joy. Suárez had signed a four-year contract and had a coach that he worked perfectly with. The Northern Irish Brendan Rodgers appreciated his style. Rodgers knew Suárez was not a static centre forward but someone who likes to move around and mix things up. He knew he wanted freedom of movement and to not have to back-track too often to cover off the defence. Suárez was convinced that with the offensive play that the ex-Swansea City manager encouraged, he could do a lot better.

Indeed, this was what happened: by 20 April 2013, Luisito had scored 22 goals and was lead scorer in the league ahead of Robin Van Persie, the Dutch Man Utd striker, who was on 21. In 43 matches with the Reds, Lucho had scored 28 times. Some of his matches were picture-perfect, like the one against Norwich on 29 September 2012, which for the second season in a row had to suffer three goals. The 2 March match against Wigan when he scored a hat-trick was one to be placed on a podium – three goals which saw him take the lead goal-scorer spot for the Reds. He was the third player to have reached twenty goals in a single season after Robbie Fowler and Niño Torres. On 10 March *El Pistolero*, with victory against Tottenham, reached a tally of 50 goals with the Liverpool shirt on his back. On 29 January in an FA Cup match against Oldham Athletic he was honoured to be able to wear the captain's armband. Steven Gerrard trusted him and the fans also.

He was considered a jewel in the crown. He had committed a few minor venal sins along the way. He had celebrated a goal against Everton by diving right in front of David Moyes, the Toffees' coach, who commented: 'Divers and theatre artists like Suárez drive the fans away from the stadiums.' At Mansfield Town in the FA Cup, he scored a handball goal. Paul Cox, the Mansfield coach, who is a kind man, did not comment other than to say: 'Suárez is a great footballer but you saw the expression on the faces of my players.' Against Stoke City, he admitted that he dived in the area, hoping for a penalty. During a match in the qualifiers for the Brazilian World Cup, the cameras caught *El Pistolero* as he gave a right hook to Gonzalo Jara, the Chilean defender. In his defence, Jara had fondled his private parts. Neither one of them was punished by FIFA.

An eventful season but nothing serious, nothing which would put him in the bad boy column of players. If anything, the achievements of his season far outweighed any minor scuffles he had had. In fact, he was shortlisted for the Professional Footballers' Association Player's Player of the Year. It was Gordon Taylor, the PFA chairman, who announced the six nominees: Gareth Bale, Michael Carrick,

Juan Mata, Robin Van Persie, Eden Hazard and Luis Suárez. The reason why he was among the select few was clear. A few prophetic words explained all: 'It would be naive to ignore the fact that he is a controversial player but this is a football-ing award. Sometimes the intensity that causes the problem can lead to victory as well. It is not always possible to put old heads on young shoulders. His footballing qualities are exceptional and outshine any problems he has.' It was Friday, 19 April. Two days later, the fall from grace, the infamous biting incident.

Liverpool were playing Chelsea at Anfield. The football-ing and non-footballing reasons made this an interesting match. Rafa Benítez, the Spanish coach who took the Reds all the way to Champions League success and the famous final against Milan in Istanbul, was back for the first time at his home after six years. He was welcomed with warm applause by the Kop.

The match was a chance to remember Anne Williams, a courageous mother who lost her son during the Hillsborough tragedy and who fought for justice until her dying day. It was a day when both teams' fans could honour the victims of that terrible tragedy and of the bomb attack at the Boston Marathon, the home city to the Fenway Sports Group. All the players had black armbands as a sign of respect. At 4.00pm, Kevin Friend, the referee, blew for kick-off. Luis Suárez was the protagonist of the afternoon for better or for worse: he played the assist for Daniel Sturridge for 1-1. Oscar had taken the lead for the Blues with a header from a Juan Mata corner. Then on another corner from Mata, Suárez jumped and deflected the ball away from goal with his hand. Penalty. Eden Hazard put it away for 2-1. However, Suárez was not done. He scored the equaliser for 2-2, which would be the final score. The match was in the dying seconds and the fans were already leaving the stadium. They heard the cheers and rushed back to show their appreciation for the number 7. Moments before, the 'incident' had taken place without anyone noticing.

It was the 73rd minute: *El Pistolero* received the ball from Sturridge, controlled it near the penalty area and wanted to turn around and head off to goal. Behind him was Branislav Ivanović, the Serbian defender for the Blues, who was stuck to Suárez like glue, as he had been all match. The ball skidded away outside of the area. Gerrard was there and crossed, Hazard punched the ball out for a corner. The TV cameras followed the Liverpool captain who had gone to take the corner, but all of a sudden all 45,000 spectators shifted their gaze to see what was going on in the box. Ivanović was on the floor. Suárez was on his feet near the goal line. He was grimacing. The referee ran over; he exchanged words with Suárez who gave a thumbs-up. The Serbian lifted up his shirt and showed the teeth marks in his right bicep. But the referee did not pay much attention to it. He was convinced the two had been holding each other. No red or yellow cards. Luis chatted to Cech, smiling, while Ivanović circled round him giving him a death stare. It was only the Sky Sport replay which showed what had actually happened. The two were fighting for the ball, pushing and shoving. When the ball finally ended up with Gerrard, Suárez grabbed Ivanović's arm and bit him. The Serb pushed Suárez away and they both ended up on the floor. Ivanović opened his arms and looked flabbergasted as if to say, 'What are you doing?'

Rio Ferdinand of Man Utd tweeted: 'He was hungry.' This was only the start of a series of jokes, witty remarks, snipes, caricatures and insults that England poured over Luis. On the net, an infinite number of Photoshopped images. They show the Uruguayan dressed up like Hannibal Lecter, the main character of Thomas Harris' *The Silence of the Lambs*, portrayed by Anthony Hopkins. Then there was *Jaws* by Steven Spielberg. 'The Uruguayan Werewolf in Liverpool', paraphrasing the John Landis film, *An American Werewolf in London*. The jokes came quick and fast: 'If you can't beat them, just eat them.' 'How did Suárez see Ivanović? Like a sandwich.'

The Sun came up with the following headline the next day: 'Same old Suárez, always eating'. The *Daily Mirror* went with 'The Kop Cannibal'. The scandal had started.

The reactions post-match came immediately. Luis wrote on his Twitter account: 'I am sad for what happened this afternoon. I apologise to Ivanović and the entire footballing community for my unforgiveable behaviour.' Later he added: 'I called Ivanović and apologised personally.'

The Chelsea defender stated in an interview for *Vecernje Novosti* a few days later: 'At the time, in the moment, you get angry but at the end of the match, the blood cools and everything is forgotten. We spoke on the phone and I accepted his apologies.'

If things appeared to have been resolved between the players, the same could not be said for the club, the FA and British public opinion. Brendan Rodgers, after having seen the images, stated that his number 7's behaviour was not acceptable. Ian Ayre, the sports director for the Reds, who had to cancel a promotional trip to the Far East and Australia at the last minute, explained that Luis was aware of what he had done, that he had damaged the good name and the image of the club. He announced that, while the verdict of the FA was being decided, Luis would be fined. The fine was paid to the Hillsborough Family Support Group.

The comments of the sporting community, opinionists and ex-footballers were not so relaxed. Mark Lawrenson, ex-Liverpool defender, stated: 'He cannot go around biting people. These things are what kids do, not adults. He is a world-class player but he gives you world-class problems.' Graeme Souness, ex-Liverpool player and TV commentator, said: 'Embarrassing. It looked like he wanted to rip some flesh off. This is worrying. I cannot see how he can stay at Liverpool.' The fans were of the same mindset. Many called BBC Radio in Merseyside to express their disgust and ask that the Uruguayan player be sold as soon as possible. A survey of *Daily Telegraph* readers approved an immediate sale of the number 7. The club did not quite see it like that: 'He is a splendid player, the top scorer in the Premier League and he has all the qualities we want from a forward. We want him to stay with us. We need to get him back on the straight and narrow and with the coach's help and that of a psychologist, we will smooth out these wrinkles in his personality.'

Some were horrified at the prospect of The Cannibal staying at Anfield. But many remembered Eric Cantona, who after having kicked a fan and served his ten-month ban, came back to play for the Red Devils in 1995.

That the incident was not that big a thing was the reaction of one individual cited in both England and Holland. This was the opinion of Mike Tyson, who in 1997 in a WBA heavyweight fight bit the ear of Evander Holyfield. In a radio interview with a US broadcaster, he commented: 'He bit someone. It happens. But I am sure that he will apologise as I did with Evander and carry on with his life.' The British Prime Minister, however, was appalled by what he had seen: 'I have a son who is seven and loves football. When players have this sort of attitude, it is a terrible example for young people in our country. As a father and a human being, I believe we should have harsh sanctions for a player who behaves like this. Yes I think so.'

David Cameron was accused of influencing the decision of the FA. The ruling for Suárez came on 24 April: a ten-match ban for 'violent conduct'. This was a harsh verdict. He was criticised on all fronts. Brendan Rodgers said that the punishment was on the man, not the incident, and a punishment with no intention to rehabilitate the player. Arsène Wenger, Arsenal's coach, was on the same wavelength: 'What went against him was his track record.' Pepe Reina, the Spanish Liverpool goalkeeper, went even further when talking to the Cadena COPE microphones: 'Luis Suárez is being treated differently to an English player. A ten-match ban is harsh and unjust. The lynching of Suárez is disproportionate. I do not justify what he has done but he knows he made a mistake. There is hypocrisy, I am not sure if there is xenophobia but that there are different standards is palpable.'

On 26 April, Luis Suárez decided not to appeal against the decision. He explained his decision thus: 'I accept that the act was not acceptable. I am not appealing because I do not want to give the wrong impression to people.' When the dust had settled, he explained himself in an interview with Uruguay TV: 'I was angry about having gifted a penalty to Chelsea. I saw red and was out of it. I do not know how to explain it but I realise I made a mistake. It is only my fault. Ivanović did not do anything to me.'

The sanction was enforced immediately. *El Pistolero* missed the last four games of the season and the first six of the next.

Sebastián Coates arrived at Liverpool from Nacional at the end of August 2011 in a transfer worth $14 million, one of the highest in Uruguayan footballing history. Lucho, whom Coates had known since the Costa Rica qualifier for the World Cup in South Africa, was his 'guide'. He showed him around the city and the club. 'He helped me settle in and that was very important to me. I was nineteen and I needed a helping hand at the start from someone like him who had already been through it. We were two Uruguayans in Liverpool. Clearly we spent time together and got on, and met up for an *asado* [barbecue] now and then.' Coates had experienced two years of controversy with Luis: 'They were difficult times, really tough for him and his family. When I met him, and you know apart from being a great footballer he is a great person, a good father, who always spends time with his kids, and a good husband, hearing all this negativity about him was not easy.'

So why did Coates think there was so much talk and accusation about Suárez in England?

'Who knows? Here in South America, we live with things as run-of-the-mill which in other countries would be a scandal or unacceptable. Just look at a match of the Libertadores Cup. There is this attitude, this habit of pushing and shoving and roughing each other up, talking back at the referee, there are lots of fouls and dives, fakes; things which in England would be disapproved of. Maybe we are used to it, not biting of course ... This tenacity is normal, it is ours. It depends on how the match is going. Luis lives each match with great passion because he wants to win. He is a player who gives everything on the pitch, he never holds back or saves himself. When the adrenalin is pumping, sometimes mistakes can be made. Luis has managed to sort his problems out and show others that they were wrong about him.'

Chapter 17

Rationality and irrationality

A conversation with Gerardo Caetano

'Luis Suárez is a rare player, a very rare player.'

This is the first comment of Gerardo Caetano, who took his time in making it. Caetano is a historian, political analyst and Dean of Political Sciences at the Universidad de la República. He is someone with a very unique curriculum. He was born in Montevideo in 1958 in the La Blanqueada area (where Suárez lived) to a family which had no interest in football. The professor was a footballer in a previous life. He played centre forward for Defensor, the third most important club in Uruguay in terms of titles won. In 1977, he played with the Uruguay U19s in the South American World Cup and then in the first World Cup for this category, with Uruguay finishing fourth. He played with Defensor until 1981 and then embarked on a university career. The reason? Caetano explained as follows: 'Football is an extremely passionate sport and there is no room for any other passion.'

The professor was sitting in his living room in Montevideo and explaining this concept in greater detail.

'Here in Uruguay the great footballers are decidedly more "classic". Diego Forlán, for example, is a classic player: ambidextrous, refined technique, superb playmaker, able to make razor-sharp passes to his teammates; he can play up front or behind the forwards to set up play. He is a classic player in that he has excellent skills and talent but he knows what he is capable of on the pitch. There are no surprises. That does not mean that his finishes do not impress you but there is always something that feels rehearsed about it, as though he has practised it down to the last detail. Suárez is completely the opposite. He is utterly unpredictable. He has an instinct to do what he needs to do to get to the goal and a feverish tension around his play that lends itself to creating unforeseeable play. He is a rare player because he is unpredictable. Forlán is more rational, he very rarely loses his rag.

'Lucho Suárez can sometimes spend 90 minutes playing his rival or playing himself. It is hard to convince him not to argue with the referee to avoid getting sent off or to not bite the defender on the other team. Everyone is watching you, five cameras pointed at you, all waiting for you to do one of your usual tricks. Lucho is the way he is. You cannot and should not change him. After Suárez bit Ivanović, when the controversy kicked off in England and everyone wanted his blood, saying that he should be forced to accept reason and be treated, Gustavo Poyet, a unique player and now a footballing expert [manager for Sunderland], said something amazing: '*Si queremos que Suárez sea Santo, lo vamos a perder.*' ('If we want Suárez to become a saint, we will lose him.') Lucho lives between rationality and irrationality which permeates a sporting event.'

Can we better explain this concept?
'Football is, *per se*, irrational. It is something that is intrinsic in the game. The supporting evidence is substantial and varied: the superstition of footballers and managers who take advice from clairvoyants and even change their formations based on what a card reader tells them. In a country such as Uruguay, where a recent survey stated that there is the

same number of agnostics as Catholics, as a youth player, I had a coach who believed that seeing a priest in a tunic was bad luck, that a beetle with its legs in the air could impact the outcome of a game, so much so that if something like this happened on the day of a match, he would change the tactics and play defensively even against an inferior team. He was convinced you did not mess around with fate. Football is full of collective and individual rituals to bless a team with good luck. Not only this: Kabbala is widely followed. After a great victory comes a great loss; it is an almost unquestionable axiom ...'

And getting back to the tension between the rationality and irrationality of Suárez ...
'There are moments in a match when the tension between reason and madness reaches a climax. Something which the spectator in the crowd cannot understand come rain or shine. The fan in the crowd thinks he has the same view of the game as the player on the pitch but the player is there in the heart of the game, engulfed by the ebb and flow of the game. I played up front. I know what irrationality is, and the irrationality of scoring a goal. I remember one time I scored an important goal. I began to run and shout like a madman. After the game, a friend said to me: "Did you realise that no sound came out of your mouth when you scored?" A goal is a punch to the stomach of reason.

'Suárez is permanently stuck in the tension between reason and unreasonableness, which he deals with by pushing for that goal, that opportunity. It is an impulse in the Freudian sense of the word, i.e. the dynamic process which consists of a push, a charge of energy, movement which drives the organism towards a goal.

'Suárez is a rare player for this reason, in the best sense of the word. He has a mental strength which is second to none. He has bucket loads of technique; he is physically fit; this kid at the height of his powers has every single footballing skill one could wish for, but his real skill is his mental strength, his complete focus when playing which can lead him to do outrageous things like biting an opponent – but at the same time it gives him this incredible ability for unpredictable moves and play which no one sees coming.

'Just look at his goals: some are classic goals, others are unbelievable. He mis-hits the ball but somehow it ends up in the back of the net. He puts himself in the most unorthodox position where even the most bizarre of strategists would not place him and sticks the ball in the back of the net; he volleys the ball off balance and instead of ending up in the stands, the ball slots in the top corner of the goal. He chases down a ball which 95 forwards out of 100 would have let go and gets a penalty, just like the one against Peru in the World Cup qualifiers. He has an innate sense of where the goal is; he can shoot without looking where the goal is. He looks for an opponent's mistake, the one that no one expected, he looks for space, the hole in the defence; he is always moving around and so he is difficult to mark. He goes into every tackle knowing that a defender can break his ligaments, as happened to me in 1976 or to Radamel Falcao [the Colombian forward who plays for Monaco], which would mean a brutal blow to his career. But he does not calculate risks, he just carries on irrationally. This is a tension which I saw in the defenders or in a few midfielders or forwards when I played for Uruguay.'

What aspects of Uruguayan football does Luis Suárez possess?
'What are the characteristics of Uruguayan football? Those that understand football in Uruguay say there are four

variables: physical ability, tactics, technique and mental ability. Information on tactics is globalised now. Nowadays there is little difference; it is very difficult to create a tactical revolution and if there is, the formations are adapted and the antidotes are found immediately. Everyone knows how everyone else plays. Before globalisation, it was not like this. You did not know much about your opponent. When Uruguay played its first World Cup match against Holland in the 1974 World Cup in Germany, Uruguay was totally unprepared and was completely caught by surprise by the Dutch 'total football'. Cruyff and his teammates could have scored ten goals. The match ended 2-0 for the sole reason that, on that particular day, Ladislao Mazurkiewicz saved pretty much anything that came near him. It is unlikely that something like that would happen nowadays. Any half-decent coach knows how the other national teams play and the characteristics of each player.

'Essentially tactics are not the determining factor and neither is the physical ability, as we are talking about a sport where you can pull together 22 players and take them to peak fitness. It is thus the technique that continues to be important. Uruguay has a mediocre team with two excellent forwards, Suárez and Cavani, but it does not have the same quality in midfield behind the wingers. It is a team that has learnt how to be compact, solid and organised.

'But the thing that really makes the difference is mental ability. Uruguayan football used to be about Charruan tenacity and cheekiness and this led to the worst ranking for number of players sent off or given a yellow card. Paolo Montero, a great footballer, was the foreign player with the highest number of sendings off in the Italian league. Óscar Tabárez, the coach, succeeded in changing this. Today, Montero is no longer a chopper like before and he has a solid mental strength. Uruguay can lose to any team but it can also beat any team. Uruguayan football has found its confidence and self-belief again. Before it thought it could not beat Brazil or European teams but now when it enters the pitch, it believes anything is possible. There isn't a player who better represents this than Suárez. They say that leading lights have to be extreme optimists because pessimists do not score. Lucho has optimism by the lorry load.'

How come Luis Suárez has become so prevalent in the Uruguayan collective conscience?
'This has never happened before. Not with Cavani, not with Forlán. It is all rather unusual. Maybe something that can help to explain this phenomenon is globalisation. Today, a fan watches Turkish football, Spanish football, Italian football, the Premier League and the Champions League and he wants to know why Uruguayans play all around the world and not in Uruguay. In Uruguay, it is a mass exodus: 200 to 300 players play outside of Uruguay. In addition, the Uruguayan championship is average. It is full of the 'old' players that come to finish their careers off and very, very young players who after one good season are off to fame and fortune abroad. Even Suárez left when he was very young. He played for Nacional but for the fans he has no ties to Nacional and is not known for playing for that team because he made it big abroad. Suárez, therefore, belongs to everyone.

'And on top of that there is the fact that Suárez is the player who scores the unpredictable and unexpected goals. When I played football, I had a dream: to score goals like Ghiggia [the goal that, on 16 July 1950 at Maracanã, gave victory to Uruguay over Brazil in the fourth World Cup]. A rare goal indeed. Ghiggia should have passed the ball to Schiaffino as in the first goal for Uruguay but instead he shot, aiming for the post nearest to him. A difficult goal, a goal which goes against any logic or reason. Illogical, like Suárez' goals which can leave you dumbfounded.

'Suárez is a bull who fights shoulder to shoulder with his opponents and never gives in. This is something to appreciate; it resonates with the history of Uruguayan football which rewards passion rather than hierarchy, bravery and refusing to give in over technical ability. Juan Alberto Schiaffino, a superb player, able to move the ball with utter elegance, never managed to conquer the hearts of Uruguayan fans because he never got stuck in on the pitch, he never looked sweaty and he did not like going in hard on an opponent. In Uruguay, football is epic and the emotional, exuberant player, the one who is passionate and fiery and goes to extremes, is raised on a platform in the minds of fans. For that reason, the hero at Maracanã is not Schiaffino or Ghiggia; it is Obdulio Varela. A tired but wise man. If you spoke to him about 16 July 1950 he would say: "If we played a hundred times, we would lose 99." He was tired of hearing about his argument with the linesman regarding his gesture with the ball under his arm. He said that he was just trying to waste time and that everything else was an urban myth. And yet he is the hero of that match.

'In general, heroes of Uruguayan teams are the midfielder, the defender, the captain like José Nasazzi, El Terrible [the Terrible], Obdulio, El Negro Jefe [the Black Boss]. The hero has never been the forward but now it is: Suárez, the dramatic player, from whom you can expect to see the unthinkable such as the "hand of God" against Ghana. There is something extremely symbolic about him because it is illogical but at the same time logical: from a no-win situation, he creates a chance for his team. It is something which he does instinctively because you can't do what he does thinking rationally. He thinks: "They will send me off, I will not play the next match, they will criticise me", etc., etc.

'In a museum in the United States, I met a man from Ghana and we got talking about Uruguay, Montevideo ... and eventually the conversation turned to Suárez. The man from Ghana butted in: "Suárez is a dirty word in Ghana." Not for us, I thought.'

Chapter 18
News from the year of resurrection

Kneeling, his shirt over his face. He was snorting and crying with rage. His dream of winning the Premier League after 24 years ended on the pitch at Selhurst Park. Steven Gerrard, who was not much better off than Suárez, took Luisito under his arm and pulled him up. Luis rested his head on Gerrard's chest and continued to cry. The captain walked away and waved. The TV cameras were too invasive. The players headed to the tunnel that led to the changing rooms. There was no way to console him. His teammates Kolo Touré and Glen Johnson tried, but nothing doing. Luis left the pitch with his shirt over his face. He knew it was over. He knew that in just two matches they had wasted the entire efforts of a season. It was the evening of 5 May 2014, the penultimate day of the Premier League. A rollercoaster of a season – emotional, dramatic, exciting and difficult, sensational and complete with summer soap opera.

Rewind to the beginning. The film is worth watching from the start without missing a scene:

29 May 2013 Luis Suárez dropped the bomb: 'I have a contract with Liverpool, I am happy at Liverpool, I love Liverpool but if there was a chance to play elsewhere, this would be a good time.' (Suárez radio interview with Sport 890) The reason was clear: after the Ivanović incident, life in England for him, his wife and his daughter had become difficult. He had suffered a lot for what people were saying about him, the English media were relentless. He could not go to the park with Delfina. He could not go out without the paparazzi hounding him. When he asked where he could go and confess, he was told there was nowhere really. There was nothing concrete but it would be hard to say no to a club like Real Madrid.

30 May 2013 The first page of *Marca* ran a picture of Luis entitled: 'Yes I want to. Agreement between the Uruguayan and Madrid if Liverpool does not come through.' According to the Madrid sports daily, a preliminary agreement between the reps of Florentino Pérez and Pere Guardiola, Luis' agent, was a done deal. Real would have to deal with Liverpool and the £40 million break clause which tied Suárez to the Reds. Pandora's box was open. Within a few weeks, the list of those courting Luis grew. The English and Spanish press reckoned the front-runners were Atlético Madrid, Bayern, Monaco and Chelsea.

31 May 2013 'Luis Suárez is not for sale. His agents have not talked to us about this intention. The club continues to support Luis and hopes that he will honour his contract.' This was Liverpool FC's reply via press release.

11 June 2013 'Do you see yourself in white, at Real Madrid?' ribbed an *RRGol* journalist. Luis: 'I am not sure if I see myself in white, the only thing I know is that I have a contract. Any player would like to play for a great club and Real Madrid is a great club. Every player wants to play at the highest level possible in his career and Real is up there with the best but they are just rumours at the moment.' During the long interview in the Uruguay camp, he went over his English malaise again: 'Since I have been here, I have never felt at ease, they have never appreciated my style of play, my attitude, I am the one who fakes it, answers back, gesticulates and then the racism etc. They never say anything good about me.' Luis continued with an interesting anecdote: 'I was walking in a shopping centre near Manchester when three or four blokes walked up and asked for a photo. When we were taking the photo, my wife shouted and told me to come away from there. One of the kids was pretending to bite me. My wife was in tears and the kids just headed off laughing. These things build up and after a while you have had enough and just want to go ...'

16 June 2013 Spain and Uruguay were playing at Recife in the first match of Group B of the Confederation Cup, a primer for the Brazilian World Cup. Uruguay, champions of America, were losing 2-0 but *El Pistolero* drew one back in the 87th minute with a perfect free-kick. Iker Casillas dived to save the perfectly curved shot but it was too late. Uruguay did not have the time to draw level.

23 June 2013 Uruguay vs Tahiti. Luis was starting on the bench and came on in the 69th minute and found time to score two goals. It was his 35th in 67 matches. One more than Diego Forlán, who had scored 34 in 199 matches for the Light Blues. Suárez became the lead goal-scorer of all time for the national team.

30 June 2013 In the consolation final of the Confederation Cup, the Uruguayans lost on penalties to Italy after a 2-2 draw after normal and extra time. Uruguay ended in fourth place just like the South African World Cup in 2010. Brazil won, beating Spain, the champions of the world and Europe.

8 July 2013 Arsenal offered £30 million for the Liverpool number 7. The offer was rejected. The Reds were not willing to sell Luis Suárez for less than £50 million, the amount that Chelsea paid for Torres.

23 July 2013 Arsenal upped their offer to £40 million and a pound for the break clause. Arsène Wenger, the Gunners' coach, wanted Suárez but he was hoping that the situation could be resolved amicably between the two clubs. The offer from the Londoners was the only concrete one on the table. Real Madrid had disappeared. Florentino Pérez and his team were wrapped up in a deal for Gareth Bale with Tottenham. The Liverpool management did not falter and stuck to their guns. The Uruguayan player was not for sale.

24 July 2013 Three months and three days had passed since the biting incident with Ivanović when Luis Suárez returned to the Reds for a match in Australia. It was the Liverpool summer tournée in Indonesia, Australia and Thailand. At the Melbourne Cricket Ground, packed to the hilt, the crowd started shouting: 'We want Suárez!' Rodgers had to give in, and in the 66th minute Suárez was back on the pitch for the Reds. Eighteen minutes for a cameo appearance.

2 August 2013 Luis Suárez was thinking of filing a formal transfer request as Torres did to force Liverpool's hand. If it was not enough, he could take the club to tribunal. This is what the English press were saying, while reminding its readers that this is what Suárez and his agent did in Holland with Groningen to force the transfer to Ajax.

6 August 2013 Suárez to *The Guardian*: 'Last year I had the possibility to go to a great European club but I stayed here. The agreement was that if we did not qualify for the Champions League in the following season, they would have let me go. I gave my all but this was not enough to finish in the top four of the Premier League. Now all I want from Liverpool is that they honour our agreement.' At the end of the 2011/12 season, the Liverpool managers had convinced him to stay by promising that the new coach, Brendan Rodgers, would get them into Europe. Nothing doing at the end of the 2012/13 season. They were seventh in the League and 28 points behind winners Manchester United. Liverpool did not qualify for the Champions League or UEFA. Suárez argued that this was not just a simple word of honour but a contractual clause which he signed in August 2012. He claimed he was willing to go to the FA if necessary. He was 26 and he had to think about his career. He wanted to play in the Champions League. He had nothing against his teammates, the club or the fans but he wanted to play at the best level in Europe.

7 August 2013 *El Pistolero* was not training with the team. Brendan Rodgers, who had excluded him, said there was no promise and no clause which authorised him to go. He saw Luis' attitude as disrespectful to a club which had given him everything and supported him. He demanded an apology before he put him back in the team.

8 August 2013 John Henry, one of the owners of the club, reconfirmed the club's position. They would not sell Suárez to Arsenal or anyone else.

12 August 2013 Steven Gerrard stated: 'He is one of the best players in the world. I understand the interest from various clubs. But if I can use my influence to make him stay, I will. I enjoy playing with him and I do not want him to go. For Liverpool to succeed and progress we need to keep the best players.'

12 August 2013 *El Observador* in Montevideo claimed Suárez would stay at Liverpool for the following season: 'For the affection shown by the people, I have decided to stay for now.' This was the sentence attributed to Luis, who was playing for Uruguay against Japan in Tokyo. Suárez played it down and denied it. The leak from the newspaper turned out to be true and Luis stayed with the Reds. The summer soap opera was over and Luis would stay with Liverpool. The fans breathed a sigh of relief.

17 August 2013 Liverpool–Stoke City, first match of the season, and Lucho was in the stands with his family and a thermos of his *mate* drink. His team won 1-0.

29 September 2013 In the Stadium of Light, 161 days after the biting incident and the last goal against Chelsea, Luis was back and scored for the Reds, with two goals against Sunderland. He celebrated by showing a T-shirt with a picture of Benjamin, his second child, born four days earlier.

15 October 2013 Uruguay beat Argentina 3-2 in the knock-out stage of the Brazilian World Cup qualifiers. Luis scored from a penalty.

26 October 2013 Ninth day of the Premier League. At home against West Bromwich Albion. *El Salta* put three in the back of the net.

13 November 2013 'Suárez don't bite Al Nashama' (the Jordanian player's nickname) was what the banner read in the Amman stadium. Luis did not give two hoots and his team won 5-0 in the tie-breaker, thus guaranteeing a place at the World Cup.

4 December 2013 Super Suárez tortured a downbeat Norwich. This time he put four goals in the Norwich goal. One better than last time. In the fifteenth minute a lob from 30 metres which went over the goalkeeper. In the 28th minute, one from a corner taken by Gerrard. In the 34th minute, an 'olé' and a volley against Leroy Fer and another goal. In the 74th minute, a free-kick which slotted in. The superlatives and adjectives poured from the sports journalists' pens. Sky Sport said they could watch his tricks for hours. Rodgers was clear in the after-match press conference. He was on a par with Messi and Ronaldo. Suárez became the third footballer in Liverpool's history to score four in a match in the Premier League, following Robbie Fowler and Michael Owen. Liverpool were in fourth place in the League behind Arsenal, Chelsea and Manchester City.

20 December 2013 *El Salteño* signed a new contract with Liverpool. He would be earning €11 million a year, €238,000 a week. It was the most expensive contract in the history of the club. However, the Reds preferred to secure the player who had scored seventeen goals in eleven matches. Luis said: 'I am happy. My future is secure for a bit.' He explained: 'The support from the fans has been fundamental in my decision.'

21 December 2013 Two goals and an assist to Raheem Sterling for the home victory against Cardiff, and Liverpool was top of the League. Four days later it was fifth, following defeats by Manchester City and Chelsea, who took them out of the Champions League places.

28 January 2014 The derby against Everton ended 4-0 for the Reds. Suárez scored the last goal of the match and took his tally to 23. He was way ahead in the goal-scoring tally.

8 February 2014 Perhaps the best victory and the most incredible of the season. At Anfield the Reds put four goals past Arsenal in just nineteen minutes. They demolished the away team. They made the Gunners look slow and cumbersome. Wenger's men went home with a 5-1 loss to their name. It was a crushing blow to their dreams of glory, whereas Liverpool started to dream about the Premier League. Also because from that moment onwards, they strung together an eleven-match winning streak.

1 March 2014 Suárez played his 100th match with the Liverpool shirt on his back. The match was against Southampton. Suárez was on goal-scoring form again. For the last four matches, he had not scored. It was strange for someone like him.

16 March 2014 Manchester United beaten at Old Trafford, 3-0. Suárez was among the goal-scorers.

22 March 2014 Another hat-trick for Suárez, this time against Cardiff. Goal tally: 28.

13 April 2014 The match against Manuel Pellegrini's Man City at Anfield was do or die. A draw to win the League. A two-point advantage over Chelsea and four over City with two games in hand. It was against Spurs in the 1963/64 season that Liverpool, coached by Billy Shankly, went top of the league table and went on to win. It felt as though destiny was on their side. The Reds were looking good after the game against City: Philippe Coutinho at the 78th minute scored for 3-2. There were only four days left in the League title race and Liverpool had fate in its hands. It looked as though the title was there for the taking. It looked as though they had done it. There was only one team in the way of clinching the title: Chelsea, coached by José Mourinho, who were playing Atlético Madrid in the Champions League semi-finals.

27 April 2014 Afternoon. The Special One vs his disciple Rodgers (who coached the youth teams at Chelsea). Instead of one line of defence, as with Inter against Barcelona at Nou Camp in the semi-final of the Champions League 2010, Mourinho placed two. Ten men to defend the area. Mourinho was thinking about the return match in the Champions League against Atlético Madrid, for which, seeing as the away game ended 0-0, he was in with a shout. He could take a risk and play the reserves. He set his trap and Liverpool fell for it hook, line and sinker. The Reds pushed on in attack but left themselves exposed to counter-attacking. There was also the Shakespearean drama moment when Steven Gerrard, the best player on the pitch, slipped and allowed Demba Ba to score for the Londoners. Willian added salt to the wound when in the 94th minute he scored the second goal. 2-0. Mourinho was over the moon. He ran up and down and beat his chest. The winning streak for Liverpool ended here. Eleven matches and sixteen without a loss. What was worse was that destiny was no longer in their hands. Liverpool still led the table and City had three fewer points, but with a game in hand and a better goal difference.

27 April 2014 Evening. After the defeat, Suárez travelled to London, where he received the PFA Player of the Year 2013/14. He beat Eden Hazard from Chelsea and Yaya Touré of Manchester City. He was the first non-European player to win a trophy. His 30 goals in the League had made the difference. The newspapers commented that in twelve months, the pariah of the Premier League had transformed into the best player. The bad boy had got himself sorted and was back on the straight and narrow. He was in a black tuxedo and bow tie. With trophy in hand, he edged towards the microphone: 'I apologise for my English. I will try and do my best. Thanks to everyone and all the people in England. This is an important prize for me after many difficult years. It gives me great faith for me and the club. Thanks again.' There were not many who failed to agree that he deserved it. There were his critics, like José Mourinho who on the last day of the League spoke to the press: 'You [the press] have moved the goalposts because the player who has won the PFA Player of the Year today is not the type of player who would have won ten, eight, six years ago. My player of the year is that of the team that wins the title, let's say a player of City, and I would choose Dzeko [Edin]. At the start of the season he was the third forward and when the team needed him because [Sergio] Agüero, [David] Silva and [Yaya] Touré were injured or [Álvaro] Negredo was not fit, he made the difference. He scored sixteen goals and for a third-choice forward, that is outstanding.' Just Mourinho being Mourinho.

5 May 2014 Selhurst Park. Suárez's tears. In the 79th minute, Liverpool were winning 3-0. Lucho had scored and was celebrating the last goal. Liverpool were still attacking with no respite, egged on by their fans. They were trying to put pressure on City and reduce the goal average. If it went to the wire and was on goal difference, who knows? Then in eleven minutes they let in three goals: 3-3 the final score. The fans cast their minds back to the Istanbul Champions League final when the Reds were three goals down against Milan and then managed to pull back to draw and then win on penalties. This time the boot was on the other foot. The first to realise that it was over were the players. Luis Suárez could not hold back the tears. He had scored 31 goals but it made no difference. He was top goal-scorer of the Premier League but it was not enough. He was the third-highest scorer in the history of the top league of the English FA. Only Alan Cole and Alan Shearer had scored more with 34. He was joint top scorer in Europe – Cristiano Ronaldo also had 31 goals in La Liga – and all this without taking Liverpool's penalties. This was all great, of course, but what about the Premier League title?

Two days after Liverpool's slip up, City played the game in hand and beat Aston Villa 4-0. They were top with 83 points, second were Liverpool with 81, third Chelsea with 79, fourth Arsenal with 76. It was still mathematically possible to win the title. They could do it on the last day of the League if they beat Newcastle and City lost against West Ham United. Few believed in a miracle but hope was all that was left. The Reds were in the hands of Kevin Nolan, born in Liverpool and fan of the Reds since he was a kid. He played for West Ham, as did Andy Carroll (ex-Liverpool forward). Maybe they would lend a hand?

11 May 2014 In the Etihad Stadium, City was drawing. At Anfield, a glimmer of hope flickered in the distance. At the eighteenth minute, Suárez took a free-kick on the left of the Magpies' goal and lobbed Tim Krull, the goalkeeper for Newcastle. The referee disallowed the goal as he had not blown his whistle. Two minutes later a cold shower for Liverpool. Martin Škrtel scored an own goal. City were winning 2-0 thanks to goals from Samir Nasri and Vincent Kompany in the 49th minute. The Reds were still down one goal. In the end the Reds won 2-1 but the miracle did not come true. City did not slip on the banana skin and just managed to pip Liverpool to the post. The Premier League was theirs. *The Sun* wrote: 'The richest team of the Premier League has won.' Liverpool, with a decidedly less affluent set-up and focusing on young English players like Sturridge and Sterling and keeping their faith in Suárez, had managed to come second. They played offensive football which was stunning to watch (101 goals, only one fewer than City). They had achieved something they had been hungry for, and that was a place in the Champions League. Everyone would have given their right arm for such a result ten months earlier but now it just left a bitter aftertaste in the Reds' mouths. They were so close. Just one twist of fate and they would have done it. Perhaps it was destiny, perhaps it was concentration in the last few matches. In any event it was a fantastic season and the regret of a missed opportunity could not outweigh their achievement. It would be difficult to imagine that such a chance would come around again soon. The Reds were up against a Man U who were off the beat after Sir Alex Ferguson's departure, a Chelsea which was being rebuilt by Mourinho; Arsenal were a bit all over the place. And they were lucky enough to be playing a dozen matches fewer than their rivals as they were not in the Champions League.

On the green grass of Anfield, when all was said and done, the players waved to the fans. Their kids were playing on the pitch wearing the Reds' shirt. Photos galore with wives and friends. Luis held his son, Benjamin, in one hand with the Golden Boot Trophy in the other (lead goal-scorer in the League). Delfina was close by. He passed in front of the fans who saluted him.

That evening on his Twitter account, Luis wrote: 'I just wanted to say thanks to the fans who supported me this year. We did everything we could right down to the last match but the important thing is that this year Liverpool is back in the Champions League!!! I and my family would like to thank you for the special moments we have shared, the work of my teammates and the Liverpool staff have been brilliant and I hope you enjoyed it. Thanks again.'

Three days later in Barcelona, when Luis was being teased about his future, he simply replied: 'I have had a great season with Liverpool and now I am thinking about the World Cup.'

Chapter 19

The stairs

A conversation with Óscar Washington Tabárez

It was a nice day. It was deep into autumn but on the pitches of the Uruguay training camp the sun was shining after several days of wind, rain and chilly weather. The temperature was perfect.

From Montevideo to the Uruguay sports complex it took about 30 minutes. The taxi zoomed through the woods of the Parque Carrasco and nipped along the edge of the Calcagno Lake. On through the suburbs where there were horse-drawn carts, the *chatarreros* (scrap-dealers) who collected anything they could sell or recycle. To the right, there was the white half-moon of the Carrasco International Airport. Ten minutes after having left it behind, Route 101 took you to Camino Maldonado, a road that headed out into the countryside a few hundred metres from the Uruguay complex. This was where the best players in the country trained.

A quick security check and then on to the complex. Palm trees, the national flag with the smiling sun and light blue stripes, and the FIFA flag. On one side the five training pitches, on the other low-level red housing with blue roofs where the changing rooms, training centres and massage parlours, medical centre, showers and press room were.

The press room was already teeming with people. In front of the table with the AUF and sponsors' banners there were

men at work, cameramen positioning their cameras and setting up microphones. It was a meeting for the international
media. Lots of journalists from the *Folha* of São Paolo and
the *New York Times* as well as the Argentine and Costa Rican
press. Everyone was waiting for the Uruguayan coach, Óscar
Washington Tabárez. They call him the Master not out of
respect as in the arts but simply because for fifteen years he
split his time between his two passions, football and teaching kids at the primary schools of Cerro, Paso de la Arena
and La Teja.

Tabárez was 67 years old and had a long career behind
him. He was a central defender on the pitch for South
American teams like Fenix, Montevideo Wanderers and
the Mexican Puebla. He started his career as coach in 1980,
coaching the youth teams for Bellavista. Since then, he had
managed ten clubs in four different countries, including
Peñarol, Boca Junior, Milan, Cagliari and Oviedo. In the
1990 World Cup, he was the Uruguayan coach. The team lost
to Totò Schillaci's Italy and the Master left, only to return to
coach the national team in 2006.

He was a coach who before taking on the national role
for a second time had had a long time to think about what
he wanted to do and what he wanted to change to bring
Uruguay into the modern game and to compete on an international level. He wanted to get rid of the image that it was a
team that wavered. He wanted to forget the disasters of the
past, like the failure to qualify for the 1994, 1998 and 2006
World Cups and the early exit from the South Korea and
Japan World Cups. His thought process had been condensed
into a voluminous report entitled: *Project of institutionalisation
of the process of the national teams and the training of its football
players.*

Tabárez then got the nickname of *El Proceso.* 'The Process' was a long- to medium-term task that would place emphasis on training of players, growth of new talent with focus on being humble and working as one. The project proposed a change in structure and methods to deal with the globalisation of football, which had seen lots of decent players leave the country. The Process took the team to fourth place in the South African World Cup in 2010, victory in the 2011 Copa America, and to the good results of the various youth teams. The project was updated in 2010 to take the team to 2014. It was a four-year plan like those of the past but it worked. Tabárez was viewed by many as the evangelist of football even for those outside of the footballing community.

It was almost 11.00am when Tabárez came down the corridor to the press room, limping slightly. He had had an operation on his spinal column because he could not walk any more or stand up. He was fine now but he needed to get over the surgery.

He dealt out pearls of wisdom. In football, nothing is impossible. He outlined the very thin line between success and failure. Sometimes it is so thin, it is invisible. He talked about his players and opponents and the favourites and also about television, which has 'brought about a fundamental change for the better in football as it yearns for a spectacle, a show'.

He philosophised about the role football has to play. He said it had been underestimated and under-utilised as an instrument of social integration. Politicians should focus on health and education as indicators of social well-being and yes, football could be part of this education. It was almost an hour of questions and answers with calm, dulcet and warm tones. He never digressed or went off-topic. At the end there was a bit of time to talk about Suárez. He started talking about Milan, which he coached from 1996 to 1997, and the disastrous season it had; he then talked about Barcelona and about the end of a cycle before moving on to talk about *El Pistolero*. He smiled as he recalled his first meeting with the number 9: 'I met him for the first time before his nineteenth birthday. He was exactly the same, he had the same competitiveness which he has today. He was making his way in the Primera División with Nacional. He was booed and treated harshly. His age was not an excuse. The fans wanted results. I remember talking to other coaches at the time who said, "Do you not see how many balls he loses?" I said: "You have to look at what he tries to do rather than what he fails to do. When he manages to get round a defender, it usually ends in a goal." Suárez already had the instinct of how to score, a skill which he has developed over the years.'

Let's talk about his career.
'For me Suárez is like the stairs of a large building. Every time he comes here to the training complex, step by step he gets to another level. Each time he comes back he is at another level. Nacional and then Groningen, Europe, albeit a mid-table club, the Under 20s and then Ajax, the club of Johan Cruyff. He was captain at only 21 years of age and also lead goal-scorer. For those stats alone, he should have won the Golden Boot, but the weighting of the Dutch league went against him. Many say that it is easier to score in that league but you still need to do it, and do it like he did. The Premier League is more demanding, more competitive, and at Liverpool he showed that he can still score a huge number of goals next to the best in the world.'

Did these numbers surprise you?
'No. Not at all. What surprised me was his ability to improve. He has always wanted to better himself because he wants to

win, he wants to achieve new goals. He is a stubborn mule. He knows what he wants and does not stop until he gets it. In these last few years, he has evolved and has become more responsible. The merit is all his. Even from a technical perspective. He does not just score, he helps his teammates and provides numerous assists – I lost count of the number of assists this year. He is a player who brings a lot to his clubs and to Uruguay. I am happy to have him with us.'

How do you see him at 27?
'He is experienced, mature, theoretically he is at the peak of his footballing career. He had a good World Cup and great Copa America, but he can do better.'

You said that before and after a match you speak to him. What advice do you give him?
'It is true. I do speak to him a lot. In the past even more so. Years ago I tried to build his confidence and make him understand that it was important for him and the team that he was more relaxed and composed on the pitch, that he did not always push so hard for goal, go for the kill with the other team and answer back to the referee.'

What is he like when he is here with the national team?
'Like the others. Here at the Complex no one feels or is a star. If I want to see the stars, I look to the sky.' The Master smiled and then continued: 'Luis gets angry every time he loses even a training match. He shouts at his teammates in defence. He goes in goal sometimes and when he lets one in, he gets angry. Afterwards he will not calm down until the evening.'

Óscar Tabárez continued to talk as he headed for his car and the cameramen filmed him. They needed images to pad out the reportage. They asked him to walk towards the pitch. It was an effort but the Master understood and did it.

One final question: who does Suárez remind you of?
'No one in particular. I believe he is no different than the other great players of our nation, of those who have managed to make it in Europe. What is clear is that he has Uruguayan football in his blood.' The Master paused and added: 'Luis is a warrior. Yes, he is a real warrior.'

He said his goodbyes and headed to his car. Thank you and good luck, Master.

Chapter 20

The saint and the delinquent

This period of 36 days was like an opera, a melodrama. There was pathos, disgrace, rebirth, falling from grace, divine punishment and tears. There was the chorus of an entire nation which would have not been out of place in Giuseppe Verdi's *Aida*. There was the hero, the tenor, Richard Wagner's Siegfried who could end up like Mozart's Don Giovanni surrounded by the flames of hell. A melodrama called *The Saint and the Delinquent*. The plot unravelled between Uruguay and Brazil from 21 to 26 June 2014.

Act I

Wednesday morning in May, twenty players from the national team were training on pitch four of the Uruguayan national training centre. It was the pitch furthest from the entrance. It was almost a private training session. There was just a small group of kids from one of the local children's trusts watching. Luis Suárez was there and whilst training he fell to the ground all of a sudden. The doctor, Alberto Pan, and the physiotherapist, Montes, ran over to attend to the fallen player. It was immediately clear that it was serious. *El Pistolero* got up and took a couple of steps. He was not going anywhere. He hopped on to the back of a buggy and was driven off. In the afternoon, Uruguay were training again. Suárez was not there. The journalists who were watching were not concerned as they were told by the

AUF that he was training in the gym. But Lucho was actually undergoing a series of tests to assess the gravity of the injury. The Uruguayan Football Association kept schtum 'for the safety of the player' (as it would be explained later by Wilmar Valdéz, Chairman of the AUF). Towards midnight rumours started to do the rounds on the Internet. Suárez was injured: a partial bruising of the meniscus of the left knee and on 22 May he would undergo emergency surgery. The news hit the country hard. At 8.00am on 22 May, hundreds of fans waited outside the Uruguay Clinic in Montevideo. The wind howled and the rain lashed but the fans waited for their hero undeterred. Luis Francescoli carried out the operation. He was the brother of Enzo Francescoli, a former player for Montevideo Wanderers, Olympique de Marseille, River Plate, Cagliari and Torino, and idol of Zinedine Zidane. At the end of the 30-minute operation, the prognosis was good.

At 3.30pm, Lucho, accompanied by his mother and his brother, Paolo, left the clinic by ambulance. Amid the flash photography and cries of 'Olé, Olé Lucho', Suárez, sitting in a wheelchair, gave a thumbs up. At 4.10pm, he arrived home in Ciudad de la Costa. That evening when the media circus had died down, he wrote on his Twitter account: 'Thanks to everyone for the messages of support, love and encouragement throughout the day!!! The strength of those who love me will make me work hard to be there at the World Cup. My family and I are truly grateful!!!'

The AUF explained in a press release what had happened: he was suffering after training, had undergone an MRI scan during the night and it had been decided that surgery was necessary. The AUF stated the injury was not serious and that he would be taking part in the World Cup. It would all depend on Suárez's healing rate. All being well he would be able to train in two weeks. Uruguay had 23 days before their first match. Over three million Uruguayans held their breath. Would he make it? The hero, the lead forward and Premier League top goalscorer might not be there. The fans mulled over the various possibilities. An entire nation was engulfed in the fate of one player.

Luis wrote on 24 May on Twitter: 'My dream is still alive. I will be at the World Cup.' This was a message written just before a friendly match that Uruguay were playing against Trinidad and was met with a roar from the crowd at the Juan Antonio Lavalleja Stadium. Day by day, the press, the radio and the TV stations in this small South American country followed every development of the number 9. Uruguay did not talk about anything else, so much so that some called the Republic of Uruguay 'the Republic of Meniscus'. '*Los meniscos de Suárez*', a song by Henry Lagarde and Aris Idiartegaray, sung by Jaime and Zitarrosa was an instant hit. The medics, traumatologists, players and opinionists all had something to say on the subject. People remembered that Lucho in 2006, when he was still at Nacional and just before leaving for Holland, had an operation on his right meniscus. That time, fifteen days later he was already back dribbling the ball. It was not just the dates but also the conspiracy theory which concerned some. Some thought that the English were involved somehow. It was the AUF that sowed the seed of doubt in journalists' minds, in its official press release, when it stated that in Suárez' last Premier League match on 11 May, he had suffered an injury to his left knee. It was inflicted by Paul Dummet, Newcastle's number 36, in the 86th minute. Suárez sprinted up the right flank and the Newcastle player, who had just come on to cover off the threat from the Liverpool number 7 chopped at Luis, who fell to the ground. Lucho got up but was clearly in pain. Dummet was sent off. The FA subsequently reduced Dummet's ban, at which some Uruguay fans thought they smelt a rat. They thought it was a deliberate foul to make sure Luis could not play in the World Cup against England. The Uruguayans started a hate campaign against poor Dummet. The insults and death threats came from all corners. The 22-year-old Welsh player was intelligent enough not to reply to the wave of hatred that came his way. He told the *Daily Mirror* that the foul was not intentional and that he hoped Suárez would get better soon and be fit for the World Cup. The English fans suggested that if Suárez ended up not playing in the World Cup, then Dummet should be knighted. *The Sun* ran riot with the story. Next to a picture of Lucho with a hood on and in a wheelchair coming out of hospital, they wrote: 'Get well (soon) slowly Luis. Love from The Sun xxxx (But looking forward to seeing you back in August).'

A tabloid hack tried to present the newspaper to the Uruguayan Embassy in London so that it could be sent to Suárez but he was politely asked to leave.

A few days later, *The Guardian* interviewed Suárez, who told the paper about his long and difficult days after the operation. Emotionally and psychologically, he was fine because he had always known deep down that he would make it to the World Cup. He did not want people in his country to remember Uruguay only for South Africa 2010. He wanted Brazil 2014 to be a memorable World Cup for Uruguay. His knee was better but he did not know how it would behave on the pitch. Was there any pain? He was dealing with it just as he did when he was knocked over by a car when he was twelve near Gran Parque Central. He fractured his fifth metatarsal but still managed to carry on playing, even with his cast! *El Pistolero* was confident that the rehabilitation in the gym at the national training facility and at the home of Walter Ferreira, the physio, was working and he was getting better. He was so confident that on 6 June he was on the pitch. His teammates had just finished training when Lucho, with two physical trainers, José Herrera and Sebastián Urrutia, walked, stretched and trotted around for a few minutes. On 12 June, he started to train with the rest of the team. It was looking good for the Costa Rica match. But at Fortaleza on 14 June Luis was on the bench. He had to endure the loss from the sidelines.

The match had started well for the Charruan warriors with a penalty from Cavani. But Joel Campbell equalised with a powerful left-foot shot. Oscar Duarte headed home for 2-1 for the *Ticos*. Marcos Ureña finished off proceedings right on the whistle: 3-1 the final score.

It could not have gone worse. 'Dreams have been turned into nightmares,' wrote the Uruguayan papers. Costa Rica, on paper, were the easiest team in Group D, the 'group of doom', which had two heavyweights, 1966 World Cup winners England and four-time winners Italy. The Master Tabárez knew he had missed out on three crucial points to get through to the last sixteen. He knew that any credit he had built up had been wiped from Uruguay's card. They would have it all to do against England. He commented: 'We need to get back on track with our weapons loaded'. One of his weapons was Suárez. He continued: 'He is no longer injured, otherwise he would not have been able to sit on the bench. He has passed all the tests and his rehabilitation is on course. He has been training and we will see when he can return. He is a key player, everyone knows that. He has not regained his match rhythm which is why he was not playing today. There are four days before the England match. If he is OK, we will think about playing him.'

Act II

Saint Luis, Holy Ghost Suárez, Luis IX, Superman Suárez, *El nuevo prócer* ('the new hero') – or rather the Liberator, like José Gervasio Antigas. The hyperbole surrounding the Uruguay number 9 was endless and was reeled off like the prayers of the rosary. *El Pistolero* was back. After 28 days away, he would lay ruin to the Three Lions. It was payback for all the criticism which he had received in England. He got Uruguay dreaming again. Nicolas Lodeiro got proceedings going with a counterattack on the left with Cavani, who waited before releasing the perfect cross to Lucho who with a header put the ball past Joe Hart, the England goalie. 1-0. Luis shot his guns in the air and laughed. *El Pistolero* ran to the bench and hugged Walter Ferreira, 'El Manosanta', the physio, pointing at him wildly. Without him, Suárez would not have been there. The physio, who was fighting cancer and alternating physio sessions with Luis with chemotherapy and who right until the last moment did not know whether he would be able to travel with Uruguay to Brazil, had made the impossible possible. Wayne Rooney brought the scores level in the 75th minute. The Three Lions breathed a sigh of relief. It was not to last. With seven minutes to go, Suárez finished the Whites off from a Muslera long hoof which Gerrard (of all people) deflected into the path of El Salta. Luis did not need asking twice. He hustled past Cahill and scored what can only be described as an immaculate finish. A cannonball which Hart did not even see. Suárez was off a few minutes later: cramp, which had set in 20 minutes earlier …

In the Corinthians Arena in Sao Paolo a sea of light blue burst forth around the stadium. The result meant that Uruguay would go through if they could beat Italy in their final group game. England, who had lost in their first game against the Azzurri, were now almost out.

Luis Suárez ran over to console his Liverpool captain, Steven Gerrard, who was playing his last World Cup: for him it was a complete disaster. Luis declared after the match: 'I need to rest and then I will start thinking about Italy, which will be tough. The important thing is we won. We had to win.' He said he had dreamed of a match like this. Taking out some stones from his boots, he quipped: 'Their coach [Roy Hodgson] said we had a player who was 50 per cent fit and that I had to prove myself in a World Cup. Today I gave them the answer.'

In the press round-up, most journalists could not leave the 'biting' and 'teeth' issues alone: 'Kicked in the teeth' (*Daily Mirror*); 'Luis Suárez (of course) takes a huge bite out of England's hopes by winning a crunch game for Uruguay' (*The Independent*); 'All bite on the night' (*The Guardian*); and 'It had to be chew!' (*The Sun*).

Omen or what.

Act III

'Chiellini seems to have been hit by Suárez. A headbutt, er yes ... a headbutt. I don't think anyone saw it. The art of provocation of Suárez.' This was how the Italian commentators described the Suárez–Chiellini incident. It was 24 June in Natal, the 78th minute of the Italy–Uruguay match, the last match in Group D. The Italians just needed a draw to finish second behind Costa Rica. The Uruguayans had to win to get through. The match was at a stalemate at 0-0. The Italians were down a man as Claudio Marchisio had been sent off in the 57th minute for a foul on Arévalo Ríos. Tabárez put Stuani on up front, taking off Pereira, a defender. He was hunting a goal. In the 65th minute Suárez had the chance to land the guillotine blow. He was in front of Buffon alone but the shot was saved by the Italian keeper. Italy were suffering.

The Azzurri locked down in defence and prepared to tough it out. This was when the incident happened. The ball was in the air and then launched back upfield but ended with Stuani in the area. Cavani appeared on the left side. Buffon had already raised his hand in the area. There were two players on the floor. What was going on? Suárez was holding his teeth and looked in pain. Chiellini was holding his arm and calling the ref. What the hell was going on? The replay showed that the Uruguayan number 9 had run toward Chiellini waiting for a cross and then run into the shoulder of the defender from Juventus who reacted with an elbow in Suárez' face. At first it looked like a headbutt as the Italian TV commentators had said. Lucho was soon to be in the firing line.

The idea that Suárez had bitten Chiellini started to do the rounds. Chiellini shouted in Spanish and lowered his shirt to show the teeth marks. He went crazy and was shouting at the ref. Ramírez, the Uruguay number 18, asked Chiellini to cover up. It looked like it was going to be a storm in a teacup. The match carried on. The Mexican referee, Marco Rodríguez, did not see or hear anything and so he did not consider it worthwhile sending Suárez off or giving him a yellow card. Italy were on the ropes and in the 81st minute the KO blow came. Diego Godín cleared everyone and the ball went in. Buffon could do nothing: 1-0 Uruguay. Last sixteen here we come. Suárez would not be there, however.

Chiellini gave his view after the match: 'The bite? It is clear, it was clearly there, whatever the ref says; unfortunately he should have blown and given him a red card. There was also a clear fake by Suárez afterwards, a clear sign that he had done something that was not right. The referees say that they should read up on players and Suárez has a clear history. The truth is that they want to protect the champions.

FIFA wants its stars on the pitch. Let's see if they are brave enough to use the TV evidence against him. The ref saw the bite but did nothing.'

Suárez gave his version of events to Uruguay's Channel 10: 'They are situations which happen on the pitch, there is no need to pay too much importance to them. We were both in the area, he hit me with his shoulder and I caught it in the eye.'

Óscar Tabárez was asked the same question again and again in the press conference: 'I would like to see the TV images. I have not seen them. If it did happen, even the referee did not see it. Therefore, it does not need commenting on. This victory is more important than one single event.'

That was not the end of it. An English journalist took up the charge. The question was whether the coach was aware that FIFA could ban the number 9 player. Tabárez's expression was not that of a happy man: 'Suárez has been the subject of criticism for non-footballing reasons and not for what he does on the pitch. He has made mistakes and has been banned but I think there are people out there who are against him. There are people who are waiting outside that door and waiting for something to happen.'

Cesare Prandelli, the Italian coach, handed in his resignation after the match, after his team's defeat and early exit from the World Cup. The Chairman of the Italian FA, Giancarlo Abete, did the same. They had other things to worry about. Prandelli cut any questions on the incident short. He did not see it, just the marks on Chiellini's shoulder. He criticised the referee but not the bite.

FIFA now came to the fore. Ségolène Valentin, the spokesperson, announced: 'The referees will be heard, all aspects will be considered and, if appropriate, a decision will be taken.' At first a ban seemed unlikely. What the punishment would be was hard to decipher. In the World Cup, there have been many unfortunate incidents over the years, from Zinedine Zidane's headbutting of Marco Materazzi in 2010 to the spitting at the referee by Iraqi player Samir Shaker in 1986 in a game against Belgium (that incident cost the player involved a yellow card and a year's ban). But TV-induced sanctions had only occurred once before. In 1994 in the United States, in the quarter-finals between Italy and Spain, Mauro Tassotti, the Milan defender, elbowed Luis Enrique, breaking his nose. The referee did not punish him at the time of the incident. The Azzurri got through to the semi-finals but FIFA saw the replay and decided to disqualify Tassotti for seven matches. Would it be the same this time round? What was certain was that the AUF could submit evidence in defence before 5.00pm (Rio de Janeiro time) on 25 June.

The day after the incident the media circus were all over it like a rash; accusations here, arguments in defence there. The Italian newspapers were not too harsh with Suárez. Sure, the bite was in the papers on the front page and the *Gazzetta dello Sport* labelled him '*Signore dei morsi*' ('King of the bites'), worse than Tyson, but the attention was focused on the weak Italian squad and the early shower for the Azzurri. Their World Cup was over. The country was disappointed with a team that had not lived up to its expectations. The dream was over. The papers who really had it in for Suárez were the English ones: '3 bites and you are out'; 'Jaws III'; 'Make biter Suárez a pariah' and 'Ban this monster' were just a selection of the witty and not-so-witty UK headlines on the incident. *The Guardian* went with: 'Suárez wrote his name into World Cup infamy'. The *New York Post* was funnier with 'Eataly'. On the net, the memes, caricatures, Photoshopped images, jokes and one-liners which came thick and fast, piling up on top of the ones from last time: Suárez as Hannibal Lecter, a figure of Chiellini with a bit missing, Suárez as the lead in the *Walking Dead* series, Suárez with a dog collar. A marketing campaign for McDonalds Uruguay saw them tweet: 'Hola @ luis16suarez, if you're hungry come and take a bite out of a BigMac'. Snickers used the photo and the line: 'More satisfying than an Italian'. Specsavers jumped on the bandwagon with the slogan 'He should have gone to Specsavers' beneath a photo of Chiellini with a red cross and a photo of cannelloni with a green tick.

In Uruguay, there was not much laughing going on. Since the rumours that Suárez was going to be banned had started circulating, the mood was black, dark black in Uruguay. For the most part, Uruguayans stood behind their man. They denied there was any 'incident'. Pepe Mujica summarised as follows: 'I did not see a bite. It seems that there is a real witch hunt against Suárez. I was taught that in football the decision of the referee should be honoured and in this instance the referee did not see anything wrong. Suárez has to put up with all sorts of incorrect behaviour during matches and he never complains because he is a warrior. If he plays for the national team it is because he is an excellent player, we do not expect him to be a philosopher or a lord.'

This was more or less the same line of defence which he had taken in the Evra case. More or less the same theory that the AUF applied in its seventeen-page dossier defending their man, which they submitted to the FIFA disciplinary committee.

The AUF alleged that there was no biting of Chiellini: 'The images show that it was a simple contact.' The AUF requested an examination of the Italian defender's left shoulder. Jorge Barrera explained: 'We have some images of a possible injury in that area and we want to know if they were taken before or after the match with Uruguay.' This defence was put forward by Suárez who denied the bite to his teammates in the changing rooms and stated it was contact with his head.

There were also those who accepted it was a bite. They did not approve of his behaviour but deemed any sanction inappropriate. They sought to explain the 'hunger' of the number 9 player with the help of psychologists and psycho-analysts. Carlos Ferrés, a sports psychologist, wrote in *El Observador* of Montevideo that the aggressive impulses which Suárez has could derive from his childhood or his adolescence. He stated that biting his opponents 'is a reaction, a repetition and non-adaptive behaviour' and that 'Suárez is a star. He is a high-performance athlete who is not "normal". He is outside the norm. But he is a human being and losing control is just a matter of time. We can all lose control when we are subjected to high-risk conditions.' The analysis which Tom Fawcett of Salford University gave to the BBC in April 2013 after the Ivanović incident was trotted out: 'The early years of a person's life help form your personality. If we look at Suárez, he had a tough childhood, during which he had to struggle to get ahead, he had to be smart. If it's happened before, it will happen again, because despite any help he receives, he will do it again.'

The child trauma theory was even upheld by Lila Píriz in an interview with AFP. Suárez' grandma said she did not know what had happened to her '*negrito*' and did not know why he had these impulses: 'maybe [it's because of] his parents' divorce and the deprivation he had to go through'.

Across the ocean in England, the analysis was relentless and all the possible reasons behind these impulses were looked at. From Freud to Kinsley, to looking at FBI reports which set out the various categories of violent biters. Theories

varied wildly from sadomasochistic fantasies to popular culture such as vampires, cannibalism to sex; from childhood to
tribal aggressiveness in football and even to war metaphors.
Patricia Ramírez, sports psychologist, wrote in *El País* of a
disorder in controlling impulses, a psychological disorder
behind behaviours such as pyromania and kleptomania. The
inability to control one's aggressiveness in the face of stimuli.
She continued saying that a person needs to be educated to
reflect before acting so that he/she has a different reaction
which allows them to deal with their anger in a different way.

There were also those who were not focusing on Suárez. A
small minority had it in for Chiellini, such as Diego Lugano
who stated: 'As a man, he is a total disappointment. I admired
him. It is not normal in Italian football that a player leaves
the pitch crying and accusing another player like that.'

The behaviour of the Uruguayan number 9 was simply
a gesture of manliness as a reaction to the whingeing and
whining of the Italians.

Just after 11.00am on 26 June 2014, FIFA made its
announcement. A nine-match ban at international level
and a four-month ban generally, plus a fine of 100,000 Swiss
francs. The disciplinary committee said that Suárez had
breached article 48 (aggressive and violent conduct) and
article 57 (act of unsporting behaviour towards another
player) of the FIFA disciplinary code. The sanction was appli-
cable with immediate effect. Suárez would miss the match
against Colombia in the last sixteen. If Uruguay exited the
World Cup, the forward would miss the next eight official
matches. The four-month ban meant that Suárez would not
be able to take part in any footballing activity be it adminis-
trative or sporting as required by article 22 of the disciplinary
code. According to article 21, during the ban Suárez would
not be able to access the stadiums where Uruguay play. Not

only that: he would have to leave the Uruguay training camp at Sete Lagoas. Claudio Sulser, Chairman of the committee, commented on the sanction thus: 'Such behaviour cannot be tolerated on any football pitch, and in particular not at a FIFA World Cup when the eyes of millions of people are on the stars on the field.'

In Montevideo, the news was received like a punch to the stomach. The country was paralysed, shocked and in a state of disbelief. No one had expected it. It was the most severe sanction ever to be applied in a World Cup. A tsunami of comment and reaction swept the nation, from players to politicians, to rivals, the list goes on. Diego Lugano was one of the first to vent his spleen on Twitter: 'Indignation, help-lessness, these are the feelings I believe we all feel. We would all like to live in a fair world but this is a world that does not exist. What happens, happens; the strong will remain the strong: the law is not the same for everyone. A hug to Luis who will bounce back as always; my thoughts go to his fam-ily who are suffering as he is: he must continue to be proud of himself, he deserves it. It does not change things: we will carry on with pride and unity, acknowledging our mistakes but with our heads held high.'

Diego Maradona expressed his opinion on the Venezuelan channel, *Telesur*: 'Who did Suárez kill? This is football, there is contact. Why don't they just handcuff him and send him straight to Guantánamo'.

Fred, the Brazilian forward, stated in a press confer-ence: 'Suárez could not deny that he made a mistake but, as a player and a human being, I understand that in those moments your nerves are on edge and the fight for space in the box is intense. The sanction seems a bit too harsh and unfair.'

Ronaldo, the ex-Brazilian striker, did not see it like that:

'Football has to maintain that line of respect and act as an example. Those that cross the line need to be punished.'

Giorgio Chiellini, the biter's victim, forgave Suárez and criticised the decision: 'Now inside me there are no feelings of joy, revenge or anger against Suarez for an incident that happened on the pitch and that's done. I am just angry and sorry we lost the match. My only thought is for Luis and his family because they have to face a tough time now. I always considered the decisions of the disciplinary committee unequivocal but at the same time I believe the sanction given is a bit excessive. I sincerely hope that he will be allowed to at least stay close to his teammates during the matches because such a ban really cuts you out.'

The Uruguayan politicians went to town on the sanction. Mónica Xavier, Chairman of Frente Amplio, tweeted: 'A shocking decision by FIFA. Come on Uruguay. We are all with you Suárez!!' Sergio Abreu, senator of Partido Nacional, wrote 'He just escaped the electric chair. One thing is a penalty and another an execution. Messrs. of FIFA: We are all behind Suárez! To win!!'

One player who did not join the chorus in defending Suárez was the Uruguayan hero from the Maracanazo, Alcides Ghiggia. He explained his views to the *Daily Telegraph*: 'Luis plays well but he has done things which are not normal for a player and for the game. Cleary his head is not in the right place. It is right that FIFA punished him. He did it in England and he has done it again. It is not normal. It is a football match, not a war.'

Luis Suárez packed his bags and left the Uruguay HQ in tears. He flew to Montevideo with Sofia and his kids. Hundreds of fans were waiting for him at Carrasco airport despite the cold. They were to be disappointed as Suárez flew in a chartered jet and was accompanied home where he would face the world in the morning. The next day he stood on the balcony of his flat with Delfina and Benj to say hello to his fans who had come together to give him support. It was 27 June and half the world's newspapers were talking about him and the ban. In Uruguay, the most used expressions were 'exile' or 'life sentence'. The papers accused FIFA of Anglo-Saxon favouritism and criticised its rules. It was not only the Uruguayans who had it in for FIFA. The Spanish papers did not hold back either. Ramon Besa wrote in *El País*: 'The sanction is not only disproportionate but it reeks of populism; it is a media show which controls football and above all its managers who make the rules and enforce the penalties which are more about news than the foul. Football's ruling body lost any moral authority the moment it did not penalise the corruption of its members and dishes out punishment without any criteria.'

The debate on FIFA's decision did not stop there. Every day a new chapter was added or a new statement came out, like the one Tabárez made in the press conference before the last-sixteen game where he said that the sanction was 'excessive' and an abuse of power and that he would be leaving the FIFA strategic committee as a sign of protest. On Saturday 28 June, Uruguay were up against Colombia without Suárez. They lost 2-0 to the Colombians. James Rodríguez had made his mark. Uruguay's World Cup was over. Uruguay had a cold winter and the presidential elections to look forward to. The Uruguayans headed home and comparisons were made to the destiny of Argentina at USA '94 – after Maradona was banned for failing a doping test, they did not perform as well.

There were 4,000 people waiting for the team. All the signs and banners were for Suárez and against Blatter. Pepe Mujica went to meet the team and on TV said: 'FIFA is a group of old sons of bitches. It is right that they punish but not that they inflict fascist sanctions. We have had to bear the brunt of a sanction which in part can be understood but not the way in which it was dealt with. It was an act of aggression against a man and his country. This is something that will stay in the minds of Uruguayans as one of the worst pages of our footballing history.' He asked the Uruguayan people not to let pain and anger be the master of reason. He thanked the warrior spirit of the Uruguayan players, thanking them for what they had achieved.

The World Cup was over but the melodrama did not end here. Penitence was around the corner.

Chapter 21

Repentance

'After several days of being home with my family, I have had the opportunity to calm down and reflect about the reality of what occurred during the Italy–Uruguay match on 24 June 2014', wrote Luis Suárez on his Twitter account.

'Aside from the fallout and the contradicting declarations that have surfaced during these past few days, all of which have been without the intention of interfering with the good performance of my national team, the truth is that my colleague, Giorgio Chiellini, suffered the physical result of a bite in the collision he suffered with me. For this:

– I deeply regret what happened.
– I apologise to Giorgio Chiellini and the entire footballing community.
– I vow to the public that there will never again be another incident like this.'

Montevideo, 30 June 2014

Chapter 22

New life

Covering your head with shame, regretting your own mistakes – this can be, sometimes, the tribute you have to pay, the route to start a new life. Or at least according to the headlines of the Catalan sport newspapers. 'He apologises, he signs', claims the front page of *Sport* on 27 June 2014, right after the huge ban for Suárez. In addition, 'FC Barcelona waits for an admission of his mistake by the player to finish negotiations'.

Three days after the apologetic tweet by the Uruguayan for 'the bite', Andoni Zubizarreta, general manager of the Catalan club, comments: 'He's showed enough strength and humility to recognise his mistake, to ask forgiveness from Chiellini and soccer in general. That's the start of the recovery process of any person who's done something badly wrong. His current behaviour says a lot about him. Apologising is not an easy thing.'

This was a sort of blessing for the predicted signing to Barcelona, a transfer commented on at length, well before his appalling gesture in the World Cup against the Italian defender. But the first who announced interest in the Liverpool number 7 were the Madrid sport dailies. Don't forget that the *Merengues* had already made their first approach in the summer of 2013 when, after the ban that followed his bite to Ivanović and the failure to qualify for the Champions League, *El Pistolero* had admitted his willingness to leave Liverpool.

And on 4 June 2014, when Lucho was still struggling with his damaged knee, *Marca* dedicated the front page to him: 'Carlo [Ancelotti] gives the OK to Luis Suárez. He's the *Galáctico* chosen by Florentino Pérez (but without letting Benzema go). The chairman offered him to the coach during a lunch on Friday. The coach gave his approval to the Uruguayan although he still considers Karim a key player.' Even if that scenario is true, it's debatable because when the coach was asked if he wanted *El Pistolero*, he was definitely sceptical. He mentioned the more than 100 goals scored during the 2013/14 season by the 'BBC' trio (Benzema, Bale, Cristiano). Don't touch a team that is performing well, that's the old football adage. Sure, Álvaro Morata, the 21-year-old striker, wants time on the pitch; he wants to play and he doesn't like being a wildcard just used for certain occasions, as we see from his transfer to Juventus in Milan, but as a replacement the Italian coach prefers a young man who still has to cut his teeth and who will accept the bench in a better mood than a figure like Suárez. Despite these arguments, *Marca* continues on this line and again on 5 June, still on the front page, it claims: '90 million. The whites get ready for a hard negotiation with Liverpool. The Uruguayan earns 10 million per year.'

That's their last broadside, as the Suárez fever, as if by magic, fades in Madrid and moves to the Ciudad Condal. It explodes right after *El Pistolero*'s comeback against England. The daily *El Mundo Deportivo* assured us that 'FC Barcelona has put the signing on track', and 'Liverpool demands 85 million but the *blaugrana* would go lower'. Next day the details of the transfer are being unveiled, with some naivety: '1. His daughter was born in Barcelona and he has relatives in Catalonia; 2. Alexis [Sánchez] could reduce the price of the deal because he's being wooed by Liverpool; 3. Luis

Enrique [the new coach of Barcelona] likes him, and he could have already given his approval.'

Euphoria for the new arrival is at its peak, but it suffers a severe setback after 'the bite'. For a newspaper like *Sport*, the transfer becomes controversial 'because the aggression calls into question the sportsmanship of the player'. Although it doesn't matter in the end, as they also say that 'the negotiations are at an advanced stage, the number 9 wants to wear the *blaugrana*. Bartomeu [Barca's president] agrees to push the boat out with a large financial offer while the farewell is assumed in Anfield. Coach Brendan Rodgers gives his OK to the operation.' And there's the official apology from Suárez that serves to downplay the issue of the bite.

Now it's just a matter of negotiations – price, payment method and possible exchanges of players. Obviously the Catalans will try to lower the cost of the player since FIFA has rejected the appeal of the Uruguayan football association and confirms the ban in its full extent. Sure, Suárez' lawyer will take the sentence to the CAS, but it is certainly true that not having Suárez in the team until the end of October is worth a little discount on the price. On 2 July, there's a meeting in London between Raúl Sanllehí, Barça's head of football management, and Liverpool's chief executive, Ian Ayre, a meeting described as productive by the Reds. Just some loose ends remain, but the deal looks almost done.

Many shops already begin to stock *blaugrana* shirts with the name and number 9 of the great Uruguayan. The bandwagon of business in football does not stop – for that there are no bites, no suspensions, no financial rights and wrongs. The negotiation reaches its conclusion punctually. On Friday 11 July 2014, shortly after 1.00pm, FC Barcelona announces the agreement with Liverpool

FC for the transfer of Luis Suárez. €81 million is the cost of the operation according to the figures filtered by the Catalan club, with a five-year contract and a salary to match the €12 million per year that the striker was earning in Liverpool. The players they have sold, say the Barça club officials (€42.5 million for the Chilean Sánchez, finally to Arsenal, €36 million for Cesc Fàbregas, to Chelsea, and €2 million for Jonathan Dos Santos, to Villarreal), balance this expenditure, second in the history of the club only to the millions spent on Neymar.

Leaving aside the financial issues, the mind boggles, thinking of an attack that combines Leo Messi, Neymar and Lucho. 87 goals in the last season between the three of them. What their understanding will be like on the field, we'll have to wait and see, but this movie won't open until the end of October, since *El Pistolero*, if there are no changes, will miss the nine opening games of La Liga and the first three matches of the Champions League 2014/15.

But this is the future. The present is made of greetings and farewells. Luis Suárez writes on 11 July:

'It is with a heavy heart that I leave Liverpool for a new life and new challenges in Spain. Both me and my family have fallen in love with this club and with the city. But most of all I have fallen in love with these incredible fans. You have always supported me and we, as a family, will never forget it, we will always be Liverpool supporters. I hope you all can understand why I have made this decision. This club did all they could to get me to stay, but playing and living in Spain, where my wife's family live, is a lifelong dream and an ambition. I believe now the timing is right. I wish Brendan Rodgers and the team the best for the future. The club is in great hands and

I'm sure will be successful again next season. I am
very proud I have played my part in helping to return
Liverpool to the elite of the Premier League and in
particular back into the Champions League. Thank you
again for some great moments and memories. You'll
Never Walk Alone.'

Chapter 23

Zero to hero

'It's incredible, it's like a dream. A once-in-a-lifetime experience.' Luis Suárez has made history with Barcelona, winning the final of the Champions League, their third big title of the 2014/15 season after La Liga and the Copa del Rey. It is the *Blaugrana*'s second treble in five years, and Lucho has had a lot to do with his team's success. Just when they were coming under more and more pressure from Juventus in the European final, he came racing in for a rebound to more or less seal the match. It was the 68th minute and time stood still for the Uruguayan. Up to that point he had made four attempts at Gianluigi Buffon's goal.

He had found it tough to settle into the game, but after the first half hour he had got into a rhythm. At that point Barça were ahead thanks to a goal from Ivan Rakitić in the fourth minute, one of the fastest in a Champions League final. The first half ended with the *Blaugrana* just about holding on to their lead, but they quickly lost their dominance in the second half. Apart from one isolated attempt by the Spaniards, the Italians took over, with Álvaro Morata making it 1-1 in the 55th minute. In the minutes that followed they were completely in control, piling on the pressure as the match became more and more intense. In the 65th minute Paul Pogba went down in the Barça box, and for a few seconds Juve were more focused on calling for a penalty against Dani Alves than on the ball ... but it was denied and play rolled on.

Lionel Messi got the ball halfway up the pitch and went on one of his runs, ending in a shot across the goalmouth. Buffon only managed to deflect it, leaving it open for Suárez. He came charging in from the right and only needed one tap to net their second goal. He carried on running, jumping over the advertising hoardings to celebrate with the fans in front of the stands. *El Pistolero* pointed his fingers to the sky. His name would go down among the greats. He had become the third Uruguayan to score in a European Cup final, after Alberto Schiaffino in 1958 and Diego Godín in 2014. But they both suffered defeat at the hands of Real Madrid, whereas Lucho would go on to win. He celebrated jubilantly, baring his teeth.

He had barely had time to enjoy the goal when he received a yellow card for a foul on Leonardo Bonucci. During the remaining 25 minutes of the match he would be seen hitting the turf several times. In the 79th minute it was due to a scuffle with Stephan Lichtsteiner, and six minutes later he lost his footing while receiving a pass, leaving him sprawling on the ground and forcing Turkish referee Cüneyt Çakir to stop play. Just before the end of the 90th minute he was substituted, Pedro coming on in his place, and the number 9 limped gently from the pitch. He watched from the bench as Neymar scored to make it 1-3 in the dying seconds of stoppage time. It was time to party. He kissed the trophy, his teammates, his children, whomever he could get to in the stands. He tied the Uruguayan flag around his waist while the photographers chased after the priceless photo of 'MSN' – Messi, Suárez and Neymar, the Barça strike force that had scored 122 goals over the course of the season.

Luis is one of the first to talk to the press. 'You have to suffer to win these tournaments. If you don't have to go through something then it's not worth it. Luckily today we won a torturous match,' he says. And he insists to the media that the best thing about the Barça team was 'the camarade-rie, the humility, the self-sacrifice, the hard work, and being united as one since the beginning of the season'. What is the secret of their success? 'Just trying to hit our targets, match after match. But above all, having the players who can make it happen,' he concludes. In between the celebrations, he pays tribute to a squad that welcomed him at one of the toughest moments in his career, and in particular Lionel Messi, with whom he has managed to develop that special relationship that has eluded many others who have passed through the Barça camp.

In this moment of happiness, he focuses only on the positive; as does *Blaugrana* coach Luis Enrique: 'It was the right decision to trust Luis. The club paid a lot for him, but he has proven his immense hunger and his desire to win titles,' he says at the press conference after their triumph in Berlin. It is not the first time that the coach has alluded to the €81 million that was shelled out for the number 9, a figure that Suárez himself prefers not to dwell on. 'I don't even think about the amount that was paid; it would be dif-ficult to live with that.'

In just eleven months Lucho has gone from zero to hero. From his World Cup disgrace after biting Giorgio Chiellini, to winning 'everything I had ever dreamed of since I was a kid' with his new club. Looking back it might seem like it came easily, but it was a slow process, a difficult journey, punctuated by plenty of doubt. No sooner had he arrived in the Ciudad Condal in August than he went straight into a special training programme, which included sessions with psychologists in an attempt to prevent any further aggressive episodes. He was said to have symptoms of anxiety and stress, and the club was concerned about his emotional stability.

He was still subject to the FIFA ban, which meant he would miss the first few matches of the season, but despite keeping a low profile, the press still scrutinised his every move. Just as had happened with Ronaldinho back in the day, a few journalists started to comment that they thought *El Pistolero* was overweight. The debate even made it into the Barcelona press room. Coach Luis Enrique was incredulous. 'He is at his ideal weight,' he said.

It was a recurring theme for a few weeks. But fortunately, by 15 October everyone had turned their attention back to his goalscoring abilities, as he collected the European Golden Shoe for being Europe's top scorer, joint with Cristiano Ronaldo. They had both scored 31 goals in the 2013/14 season. As he held his trophy, Luis insisted he was '100 per cent ready' to close the darkest chapter in his footballing career and finally make his Barcelona debut. He only had to wait a few more days. His first official outing in a *Blaugrana* shirt was on Saturday 25 October at 6.00pm at the Santiago Bernabéu. He was making his debut in the first big *Clásico* of the season – quite an initiation.

His family were in the stands to support him in this crucial match. Despite four months of inactivity, Luis Enrique gave him a vote of confidence by putting him in the starting line-up. During the few minutes of warm-up time he practised passing with Messi and Neymar. They switched positions and took some shots at goal. Barça's new trident were finally united and ready to show everyone what they could do.

And it only took them three minutes. Suárez received the ball on the right wing and made an incredible pass to the far side, setting it up perfectly for the Brazilian. Neymar made it 0-1 – one of the fastest-ever goals in the history of encounters between the two teams.

A few minutes later, Luis fed the ball to Messi, whose

shot was stopped by Real goalie Íker Casillas. But after that, Barça deteriorated and Madrid took back the game with goals from Cristiano Ronaldo, Pepe and Karim Benzema. With the scoreline against them, Luis seemed to find another burst of energy, but the team as a whole seemed to be sagging, and he was substituted in the 68th minute. He came off knowing that he could do a lot better.

El Salteño had to wait another month before he scored in a *Blaugrana* shirt. It happened on 25 November against the Cypriot team Apoel FC in the penultimate match of the Champions League group stage. The visitors ended up winning 0-4 in Nicosia, and it was a chance for Suárez to really show what he could do. He scored the first goal in the 26th minute with a solo move that began with a backheel pass through the legs of one of the defenders, followed by a shot that sped past goalie Urko Pardo into the far corner of the net. The number 9 was euphoric, kissing his Barça wristband for the first time since his arrival – something he used to do at Liverpool when he went on to the pitch or scored a goal. It was a superstition, something to bring him luck. 'I have various wristbands,' he told club magazine *Revista Barça*. 'The red one was to warn against jealousy and the green one Sofía gave me, I used to make three wishes on it. Once in the past I had to tape up my wrist and then it brought me luck so I kept doing it.' After that he never played a match without a band, changing the colour depending on whether he played for Uruguay or his club.

Two weeks later he was finally able to shine in front of his home crowd. Barcelona were playing Paris Saint-Germain at the Nou Camp on 10 December. The two teams were fighting it out for the top spot in Group F. Ibrahimović scored first for the French team in the 14th minute, but Barcelona took over and dominated from there on in. Messi equalised almost immediately thanks to a pass from Suárez – his sixth assist in nine *Blaugrana* matches so far: 'You have to help all your teammates, that was my aim,' he would say after the match. But before facing the press, he got to enjoy an even more magical moment. In the 76th minute, after Neymar had put them in front, Luis took advantage of the rebound when goalie Salvatore Sirigu blocked another shot from the Brazilian, and netted it to make it a definitive 3-0. The crowd chanted his name as he dropped to his knees and soaked in their praise. 'He's an exceptional kid, we all know what a good footballer he is,' teammate Andrés Iniesta told *El Mundo*. 'It's clear that he will bring a lot to the side. It's great to have him on the team, we will be even better up front.' The Barça veteran shared the same agent as Luis, and was one of the newcomer's biggest fans in the dressing room.

Lucho had to wait until Christmas to score again, this time in La Liga against Córdoba. It was his eighth match and he still hadn't scored in the Spanish championship. But all that changed in the 52nd minute. Not only did he manage to score the goal he had been chasing for months, he managed to reinvigorate a dull game. Despite going ahead in the first minute, Barça had to endure whistles from the crowd throughout the entire first half. But Luis opened things up again and three more Barça goals followed, making it a resounding 5-0 victory. 'I wasn't at all fixated on it. I know I'm a striker who has to score goals, but I was sure that they would start flowing with the help of my teammates,' he said in the press zone after the match. He dedicated the goal to his wife and two children, who were unable to be at the Nou Camp but were watching from home.

A few days later he summed up his 2014. 'On a personal level things happened that were extremely difficult. But I am very happy to have joined the best club in the world.' And he said playing with Messi and Neymar was easy, 'because they do incredible things that you never imagine they could do. Once you spend time with them, in training and in matches, you are even more aware of how talented they are and what they are capable of. And they make it really easy to play alongside them.' He also acknowledged that the shift to Spanish football was not easy. 'In the Premier League, when I was with Liverpool, it was difficult to find a team who would completely box you in. You always had space to move, to go on the attack. There are strong, fast defenders, big guys or tall guys, I'm used to that. But here they are more technical and they work well together, they are very in sync. They know how Barça can dominate so there are times when they make it very difficult for you to move.'

The Uruguayan was starting to settle in after several months trying to find his place on the pitch. First, coach Luis Enrique put him on the far right, but in the end he moved him into the number 9 position, and it was there that the Suárez–Messi–Neymar trident began to work. But was the coach really the one who made it happen? According to something that came out later in a radio interview, maybe not. 'One day I moved into the number 9 position and Messi told me to stay there,' said Luis. 'Then the coach saw that we had found a good solution and he started to test it out.' His words caused a stir in the dressing room, but Luis Enrique cleared things up with a somewhat sarcastic explanation: 'Yes, the players always choose who goes where, who gets to play, who starts, what formation or strategy we're using and how much to push forward. It's normal for the players to decide all that stuff – if we win. If we lose then I'm the one who decided.'

It was not the first example of Leo's power in the dressing room, but it was a rare occurrence for the Argentine to find such synergy with another striker. He had adapted well with Neymar, but his bond with *El Pistolero* seemed to extend beyond the football pitch. 'We understand each other very well both on and off the pitch,' said Leo. 'I think a good relationship off the pitch helps things on the pitch.' And it was partly thanks to *mate*, the caffeine-rich tea that neither Uruguayans nor Argentines can do without, as well as the South American-style barbecues at Javier Mascherano's house. 'Getting together to drink *mate* always brings people closer. That's what brought Leo and me together at first,' explained Luis. 'But I was made to feel incredibly welcome by the entire team.' It wasn't instantaneous, but by the end of the year the relationship had been cemented. 'You feel more comfortable over time. The fact that he's Argentine and I'm Uruguayan made it easier. There will always be rivalries, and a Uruguay–Argentina derby will always stir up debate, but here we all play for the same side. My relationship with Leo is great.' So much so that Lucho has bought a house in Castelldefels, a few metres from Messi's home. It's true that his in-laws live in the same area, but his proximity to his teammate is an indicator of their strong relationship.

But on 4 January 2015 Luis and the rest of the team were caught up in the tension that was building between the coach and Lionel. The Uruguayan found himself alone up front against Real Sociedad at Anoeta – Messi and Neymar were kept on the bench for a good chunk of the match because they returned later than the rest of the team from their Christmas holidays, despite the fact that they had express permission from the club. The *Blaugrana*, now behind Real Madrid in La Liga, lost following an own goal. It wasn't a huge defeat, but it left a poor impression nonetheless, and the players' morale was shattered. Shortly afterwards the media revealed that after that humiliation, some of them

created a WhatsApp group in an attempt to change the attitude of the team. The first message was blunt. 'If we continue
like this we won't win anything this year.' After that, things
began to improve bit by bit.

On 8 January Suárez boosted his goal tally with one in the
first leg of the Copa del Rey last-sixteen tie against Elche (5-0
at the final whistle). And on 11 January he scored against
Atlético Madrid at the Nou Camp (3-1 to Barça). The match
left a lasting image that was more significant than it may have
appeared at first: a euphoric Neymar, Messi and Lucho, running towards the crowd with their arms around each other to
celebrate the third goal, scored by Leo. It was a moment that
perfectly captured the harmony between the three stars, and
how well they had begun to understand each other.

On 28 January Luis turned 28, and celebrated as Barça's
fourth-highest scorer of the season, trailing Messi, Neymar
and Pedro. But he was still a long way behind what had been
expected of him when the club shelled out €81 million for
his transfer. The media were complaining that he still didn't
have a fixed position on the pitch, which was limiting his
goalscoring opportunities – although he made up for it with
his generosity, determination and astonishing willingness to
chase every ball. On his birthday, Barça knocked Atlético out
in the quarter-finals of the Copa del Rey. But despite their
2-3 victory, Suárez was only able to help his teammates with
their chances, he didn't make any of his own. When Neymar
was asked whether he was advising Suárez on how to adapt
to a club with as much history and baggage as Barça, the
Brazilian immediately leapt to his defence. 'He is one of the
best strikers in the world. He should be the one advising me.
He creates goals for us, he makes amazing assists. I hope to
be able to play alongside him for many years.'

In February Barça seemed to shake a leg. In their 21st

league match of the season, Luis was instrumental in their comeback against Villareal (3-2 to the Catalans). But despite contributing decisively, he was once again unable to convert any of the chances that came his way. According to Prime Time Sports's 2014–15 Soccerex Transfer Review, which evaluates the progress of the ten most expensive European signings, he had taken part in 51 per cent of Barça's on-pitch time since the start of the season. But counting just from the end of his ban it rose to 88 per cent. And he had run an average of 10.6 kilometres per match.

On 8 February he scored his sixth goal in a Barça shirt thanks to a pass from Messi, helping them beat Athletic Bilbao 5-2. And three days later the team notched up their tenth consecutive victory, against Villareal again, 3-1 in the first leg of the Copa del Rey semi-final. Suárez gifted Leo the first goal, and the Nou Camp thanked him by feverishly chanting his name.

On 15 February all his efforts finally paid off when he scored a superb scissor-kick goal – without a doubt his best so far at the club. It was the final goal of Barcelona's 5-0 white-wash of Levante, scored in the 72nd minute. He had barely been on the pitch for six minutes, after coming on to replace Neymar. Adriano crossed the ball and he responded with the overhead kick. After it went into the net, he got up and strolled over to Messi, who hugged him, while the rest of the team came racing over to celebrate with them. The cameras showed Luis kissing his right hand – first on the thumb, then on his index finger, then on his ring finger – three times on that one just in case Sofía missed it. That would become a ritual after every goal.

It was déjà vu at Manchester City nine days later. The first leg of the Champions League last sixteen was Suárez's chance to play on English soil again, although he preferred to avoid any comparisons. 'It's different now. When I was over there I was playing with Liverpool. Now I play for a different team, it will be a very different type of match. It's a totally different experience.' Barça were the favourites. 'But when you play against a great team, you never know what will happen on the pitch. They have very good players and fantastic technical skills, but we are Barcelona, we know our capabilities and we know what we can do against City.' Luis Enrique was also confident in his men, particularly Suárez. 'It's his first season at the club, but he's an important member of the strike force. He has attributes that really benefit us – he's a natural scorer who handles the ball excellently, he works well with the midfielders and is good at finding the gaps in the defensive line to go on the attack. He will make a big contribution.'

And Lucho did everything in his power to help beat the Premier League champions, scoring two in half an hour to make it 1-2 to the visitors, more or less putting them through. It was his first brace since arriving at the club. 'I don't know if it makes it more special, but it does have a certain significance after all those years that I spent in England with Liverpool,' he declared after the match. Meanwhile the British press claimed that the Uruguayan tried to bite Martín Demichelis, but he was vindicated by the replay. 'He put his hand up to my neck to block me. I don't know what they're trying to do, they just want to stir things up. Every tiny movement I make gets turned into a huge deal. They must still be hurting after what I did to them in the World Cup,' said *El Pistolero* on Uruguay radio station Sport 890, referring to his country's victory over England in Brazil.

Luis was on a hot streak. In fact, by 9 March he had moved up to being Barcelona's third-highest scorer with eleven goals, just behind Neymar and Leo. The following day they played Rayo Vallecano, crushing them 6-1 and reclaiming the top spot in La Liga with 62 points. They were first in La Liga, they were through to the Copa del Rey final after beating Villareal in the return leg (6-2 on aggregate) and they had made it into the Champions League quarter-finals after beating City 1-0 in the return leg. They were well on their way to making it another historic season. After their initial doubts about Luis Enrique's strategy, the media were now talking about the 'power of the trident', in reference to the forwards' incredible synergy.

And they were at it again on 22 March in the second *Clásico* of the season. The two rival teams headed out on to the Nou Camp pitch at 9.00pm, and Real seemed to take control. But in the eighteenth minute the locals took advantage of a free-kick to go ahead. Cristiano Ronaldo got the equaliser, but ten minutes after half-time Lucho scored, banishing the memory of his first *Clásico* five months earlier at the Bernabéu, his Barcelona debut, which had been more pain than glory. He was like a different player now; no one could deny how far he had come since then. He had gone from being incognito to establishing himself as a critical member of the team, a solid and generous player capable of sacrificing individual plaudits for the benefit of the group. He wasn't about to reclaim the Golden Shoe, but at least he had the pleasure of scoring at one of the most symbolic moments of the season. Dani Alves sent him a spectacular long pass, which he controlled on the edge of the area, before deftly shrugging off two defenders and shooting with his right foot to send the ball into the back of the net, leaving Íker Casillas in a heap on the ground. Lucho ran towards the fans, sinking to his knees in celebration, and seconds later his teammates came piling in on top of him.

It was the most memorable image of the night, as his

goal sealed the match. It was his fourteenth of the season, his eleventh since January. 'It's my most important goal so far, because of the extra significance of scoring against Real, and because it came at an important moment for us,' he said. Even Luis Enrique, not usually known for extolling individual performances, praised *El Pistolero*. 'He is not just a centre forward in the traditional sense. He is capable of reading the play and forming great partnerships, plus he is a great goalscorer and he needs very few touches to finish it off. He has brought a lot to the team since day one.' Lucho enjoyed his big moment: 'It's the best feeling when I'm helping score goals and making assists. As long as the team is doing well I'm happy.' Although he noted: 'I don't feel like I'm the best in the world when I score. Nor do I feel like I'm a failure when I make mistakes. Flattery is obviously very nice, but it can also be damaging.'

On 2 May he scored his first hat-trick for Barça, making his mark in the team's 0-8 annihilation of Córdoba. Lucho was on a roll, but unfortunately the season was coming to an end, and he would not have time to try to beat his tally of 31 for Liverpool the previous year. At least his Barça average was marginally better – 0.63 per match, whereas it was 0.62 over his three-and-a-half seasons at the English club. And although his own stats hadn't been particularly stellar in Spain, he was on the cusp of experiencing a historic moment with his new club.

But first, two moments worth highlighting. The first was rather surreal – one of those occasions that shows football at its worst, during the derby at Espanyol in the 33rd round of league matches, which Barça won 0-2. Apropos of nothing, someone threw carrots at him from the stands, shouting insults and calling him a rabbit, presumably in reference to past biting incidents and his prominent teeth. A bizarre insult.

The second, by complete contrast, showed the loving, supportive side of the game. On 6 April, just a few hours before Barcelona were to beat Bayern Munich 3-0 to make it through to the Champions League final (5-3 on aggregate), a Uruguayan cancer charity of which the player is a patron released a three-minute video of him talking to a young cancer patient on Skype. The fan could barely hold back the tears when he saw the Barça number 9. In the extremely emotional clip, Luis promised to send him one of his shirts: 'one of the ones I've played in, not one from the shop'. It revealed a completely different side to Suárez – the best version of himself.

And he showed his caring side again on 16 May, tweeting messages of support to former teammate Steven Gerrard who had just played his last game at Anfield. 'Thank you my friend for everything. You are truly one of the greatest!' The following day was the penultimate match of the championship, where Barça sealed their Liga victory at Atlético Madrid thanks to a single goal from Messi. Lucho wasn't on the pitch. He had to make do with watching from the sidelines after picking up a hamstring injury. But he was back in time for the next big clash: the Copa del Rey final on 30 May. They lined up with Athletic Bilbao at the Nou Camp to sing the national anthem, and then Barcelona dominated from start to finish. Suárez was on for 76 minutes before being replaced by Pedro. He didn't score but he played tirelessly and made a good impression, and he provided the assist for Neymar to score the second goal. Barcelona won 1-3 and took home their 27th Copa del Rey. Adriano Correia celebrated by dousing Lucho in water and the Uruguayan didn't hesitate to respond by falling down on to the pitch in jest, mimicking faking an injury.

It had certainly been the most difficult year of his career, as well as ultimately the most gratifying. 'I'm being smarter now,' he reflected. 'Things happen for a reason.'

A career in numbers

Name: Luis Alberto Suárez Díaz

Nickname: Luisito, Lucho, Salta, Tiburón, Depredador,
Pistolero, Caníbal

Date of birth: 24 January 1987

Place of birth: Salto, Uruguay

Nationality: Uruguayan

Parents: Sandra, Rodolfo

Brothers and sisters: Paolo, Giovanna, Leticia,
Maximiliano and Diego

Wife: Sofia Balbi

Children: Delfina, Benjamin

Height: 1.81m

Weight: 81kg

Position: Forward

Shirt number: 9

Teams

Deportivo Artigas, Urreta FC, Club Nacional de Fútbol
(2005–2006), FC Groningen (2006–2007), Ajax (2007–2010),
Liverpool (2011–2014), FC Barcelona (2014–)

Club Nacional de Fútbol

First appearance for first team: 3 May 2005, Copa Libertadores
match against Junior, Barranquilla, Colombia.

First goal: 11 August 2005, Ciudad del Tajo Trophy match
against Sevilla, Ronda, Spain.

First league goal: 10 September 2005, Opening Tournament
match against Paysandú in Montevideo.
34 appearances, 12 goals

FC Groningen
First appearance for first team: 20 August 2006, Eredivisie
match against Feyenoord in Groningen.
First goal: 14 September 2006, UEFA Cup match against
Partizan, Belgrade.
First league goal: 1 October 2006 against Vitesse in Groningen.
37 appearances, 15 goals

Ajax
First appearance: 15 August 2007, Champions League match
against SK Slavia Praga in Amsterdam.
First goal: 19 August 2007, Eredivisie match against
De Graafschap, Doetinchem.
159 appearances, 111 goals

Liverpool
First appearance and first goal: 2 February 2011,
Premier League match against Stoke City in Liverpool.
133 appearances, 82 goals

Barcelona
First appearance: 25 October 2014,
La Liga match against Real Madrid in Madrid.
First goal: 26 November 2014, Champions League match
against Apoel, Nicosia.
43 appearances, 25 goals (as of 15 June 2015)

Uruguay

First appearance for first team: 7 February 2007,
friendly match against Colombia, Barranquilla.
First goal: 13 October 2007, World Cup qualifier
against Bolivia in Montevideo.
82 appearances, 43 goals (as of 15 June 2015)

Titles won
Nacional
Uruguayan league title 2005/06

Ajax
KNVB Cup 2010

Liverpool
League Cup 2012

Barcelona
La Liga 2015
Copa del Rey 2015
Champions League 2015

Uruguay
Copa America 2011

Individual awards
PFA Player of the Year 2013/14
FWA Footballer of the Year 2013/14
European Golden Shoe 2013/14
Barclays Premier League Golden Boot 2013/14
Barclays Player of the Season 2013/14
FSF Player of the Year 2013/14
Copa America Player of the Tournament 2011
Dutch Footballer of the Year 2009/10

Bibliography

Books

A.A.V.V., *100 años de la Camiseta Celeste*, Tradinco, 2010

Apo, A., *Y el fútbol contó un cuento*, Alfaguara, 2007

Bassorelli, G., *Héroes de Peñarol*, Fin de Siglo, 2010

Bassorelli, G., *Héroes de Nacional*, Fin de Siglo, 2012

Cavani, E., *Quello che ho nel cuore. Vita, calcio e fede*, Mondadori, 2011

Castillo, F. and Varoli, H., *Hasta la última gota. Vida de Fabián O'Neill*, Sudamericana, 2013

Etchandy, A., *Memorias de la pelota. Más de un siglo de fútbol uruguayo*, Caballo Perdito, 2003

Fontanarrosa, R., *Puro fútbol*, Ediciones de la Flor, 2000

Galeano, E., *Fútbol a sol y sombra*, Siglo veintiuno de España editores, 1995

Garrido, A., *Maracaná: La historia secreta*, De Autor, 2012

Holt, N., *The Mammoth book of the World Cup*, Robinson, 2014

Kuper, S., *Ajax: The Dutch, The War*, Orion, 2011

Kuper, S., *Calcio e potere*, Isbn Edizioni, 2008

Lissardy, A.L., *Vamos que Vamos. Un equipo, un país*, Alfaguara, 2011

Luzardo, A., *Campeón de los tres siglos*, Fin de Siglo, 2011

Maiztegui Casas, L., *Orientales, Una historia política del Uruguay*, 1-2-3-4-5, Planeta, 2005–2010

Morales, A., *Fútbol, identidad y poder 1916–1930*, Fin de siglo, 2010

Peace, D., *Red or Dead,* Faber and Faber, 2013

Prats, L., *Goles y Votos,* Fin de Siglo, 2013

Reyes, A., *El proprio fútbol uruguayo,* Palabrasanta, 2012

Risso, E. and Trujillo, V., *Nacional 88 ,* Fin de Siglo, 2013

Riva, E., *Ladislao Mazurkiewicz. El arco, su mundo,* Fin de Siglo

Sacheri, E., *La vida que pensamos. Cuentos de fútbol,* Alfaguara, 2013

Vence, E., Peñarol. *Serás eterno como el tiempo ... El comienzo de la Gloria,* Banda Oriental, 2013

Viglietti, H., *De corazón celeste Diego Lugano,* Planeta, 2011

Viola, W., *Celeste Inmortal,* De la Plaza, 2014

Wernicke, L., *Historias insólitas del fútbol. Curiosidades y casos increíbles del fútbol mundial,* Planeta, 2014

Williams, J., *Red Men: Liverpool Football Club The Biography,* Mainstream Publishing, 2011

Wilson, J. and Murray, S., *The Anatomy of Liverpool. A History in Ten Matches,* Orion, 2013

Newspapers

Uruguay:

El País

El Observador

La Republica

Últimas noticias

Ovación

El Pueblo

Cambio

La Prensa

Argentina

Clarín

Olé

Holland

De Telegraaf

De Volkskrant

Dagblad Van Het Noorden

UK

The Times

The Guardian

The Independent

Daily Mirror

Daily Star

Daily Telegraph

The Sun

Liverpool Echo

Spain
El País
El Mundo
Abc
La Vanguardia
El Periódico de Catalunya
Marca
As
Mundo deportivo
Sport

Italy
Corriere della Sera
La Repubblica
La Gazzetta dello Sport
Corriere dello Sport
Tuttosport

France
Le Monde
Libération
L'Équipe

USA
The New York Times

South Africa
Sunday Times
Daily Sun

Magazines
FourFourTwo (England)
World Soccer (England)
France Football (France)
So Foot (France)
El Gráfico (Argentina)
Panenka (Spain)
Placar (Brazil)

TV/other media
Canal 5 (Uruguay)
BBC (England)
Sky Sports (England)
Canal+ (France)
Rai (Italy)
Fox Deportes (Argentina)
ESPN (Argentina)

TV programmes
Trotamundos, Amsterdam a Liverpool, Monte Carlo Televisión (Uruguay)

Films
Maracaná, la película, directed by Sebastián Bednarik and Andrés Varela, 2014.
'*3 Millones': La aventura Celeste contada por los Roos*, directed by Jaime Roos, Yamandú Roos, 2011

Music

A.A.V.V. Uruguay, *Campeón de America*, Montevideo Music
    Group, 2011
Jaime Roos, *Clásico: Todos sus Hits*, Bizarro, 2007

Websites

www.fifa.com
www.uefa.com
www.auf.org.uy
www.urretafc.com.uy
www.nacional.com.uy
www.fcgroningen.nl
www.ajax.nl
www.liverpoolfc.com
www.luissuarez.co.uk
www.facebook.com/suarez16luis
https://twitter.com/luis16suarez

Acknowledgements

Thanks to Sergio Suárez, Lila Píriz, Atasildo Suárez, Gladys Fernández, Alfredo Honsi, Mario Delgado Aparaín, Carlo De Pena, Juan Cruz Mascia, Sebastián Coates, Mathías Cardaccio, Braian Rodríguez, Eduardo Ache, Wilson Píriz, Ricardo Perdomo, Martín Lasarte, Bruno Silva, Óscar Tabárez, Gerardo Caetano, Lincoln Maiztegui Casas, Jaime Roos, Rubén Sosa, Mario Romano, Ricardo Artigas, Florean Neira, Daniel Silveira, Diego Tabáres, Freddy Bernárdez, David Endt, Tom Egbers, Ronald de Boer, Gabri, Henk Mulder, Pino Camera, Hugo Alves Velame, Hermen Pinkster, Needet Kul, Henk ten Cate, Duncan Heath, Robert Sharman, Charlie Wright, Roberto Domínguez, Laure Merle d'Aubigné and Lorenzo Caioli.

Dedicated to Elvira, Magdalena, Violeta, Julieta, Eduardo, Olmo, Tullio and Alda.